Best Easy Day Hikes Series

Best Easy Day Hikes
Adirondacks

Third Edition

Lisa Ballard

FALCONGUIDES

ESSEX, CONNECTICUT

To my son, Parker Densmore, my favorite hiking pal!

FALCONGUIDES®

An imprint of Globe Pequot, the trade division of
The Rowman & Littlefield Publishing Group, Inc.
4501 Forbes Blvd., Ste. 200
Lanham, MD 20706
www.rowman.com

Falcon and FalconGuides are registered trademarks and Make Adventure Your Story is a trademark of The Rowman & Littlefield Publishing Group, Inc.

Distributed by NATIONAL BOOK NETWORK

British Library Cataloguing-in-Publication Information Available

Library of Congress Cataloging-in-Publication Data

Names: Ballard, Lisa Densmore, author.
Title: Best easy day hikes Adirondacks / Lisa Ballard.
Description: Third edition. | Essex, Connecticut : FalconGuides, [2024] |
    Series: Best Easy Day Hikes series | Second edition published in 2017. |
    Summary: "Best Easy Day Hikes Adirondacks, Third Edition, features the
    best easy day hikes throughout the area. With detailed maps and trail
    descriptions, navigating these trails is made easy. It's the
    perfect tool for day hikers, families, and local outdoors people looking
    to explore the Adirondacks in an easy day hike. In addition to
    information on the trails themselves, this guide includes GPS
    coordinates, as well as a section on regional attractions, lodging and
    dining, and other noteworthy public lands well-suited for outdoor
    adventure. It is also filled with useful information on the area's
    history, geology, fauna, and flora"—Provided by publisher.
Identifiers: LCCN 2023051344 (print) | LCCN 2023051345 (ebook) | ISBN
    9781493077748 (paperback : acid-free paper) | ISBN 9781493077755 (epub)
Subjects: LCSH: Day hiking—New York (State)—Adirondack
    Mountains—Guidebooks. | Hiking—New York (State)—Adirondack
    Mountains—Guidebooks. | Walking—New York (State)—Adirondack
    Mountains—Guidebooks. | Trails—New York (State)—Adirondack
    Mountains—Guidebooks. | Adirondack Mountains (N.Y.)—Guidebooks.
Classification: LCC GV199.42.N652 A354 2024 (print) | LCC GV199.42.N652
    (ebook) | DDC 796.5109747/5—dc23/eng/20240105
LC record available at https://lccn.loc.gov/2023051344
LC ebook record available at https://lccn.loc.gov/2023051345

♾️™ The paper used in this publication meets the minimum requirements of American
National Standard for Information Sciences—Permanence of Paper for Printed Library
Materials, ANSI/NISO Z39.48-1992.

Best Easy Day Hikes
Adirondacks

Help Us Keep This Guide Up to Date

Every effort has been made by the author and editors to make this guide as accurate and useful as possible. However, many things can change after a guide is published—trails are rerouted, regulations change, techniques evolve, facilities come under new management, etc.

We appreciate hearing from you concerning your experiences with this guide and how you feel it could be improved and kept up to date. While we may not be able to respond to all comments and suggestions, we'll take them to heart, and we'll also make certain to share them with the author. Please send your comments and suggestions to the following email address:

> Falcon Guides
> Reader Response/Editorial Department
> Falconeditorial@rowman.com

Thanks for your input, and happy trails!

Contents

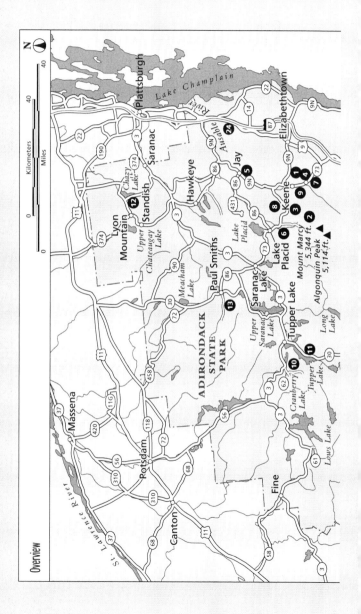

Overview

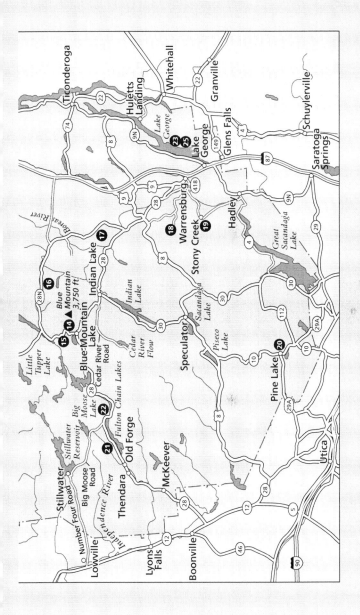

Acknowledgments

I am often asked to name my favorite hikes in the Adirondacks. My favorites are not due to the nuances of the trail or the views—they are exceptional because of the friends and family who accompanied me: my husband, Jack Ballard; my son, Parker Densmore; my stepdaughter, Zoe Ballard; my brother Wayne Feinberg, his daughter Hannah, and her husband Adam; my cousin Gene Bergman and his sons Woody and Elijah, their wives Alley and Megan, and Elijah's son Caleb; and my friends, Peggy Shinn and her daughter, Samantha, Lyndon and Ilyse Tretter, Win and Mundy Piper, Helena Haase and her son and daughter Max and Emma, and Liz Venesky, all of whom hiked with me while I was updating this book. Thank you for exploring the Adirondacks with me.

I also owe my sincerest gratitude to Peter Sachs at Lowa. Thank you for your sense of humor and for keeping my feet happy day after day on the trail.

And last but certainly not least, I would like to thank the New York State Department of Environmental Conservation, the Adirondack Mountain Club, the Adirondack Trail Improvement Society, and the Adirondack Mountain Reserve for their maintenance of the many paths I followed. With over 2,300 miles of trails in the Adirondack Park, it's a mammoth task, but you help make the Adirondacks a special place to visit.

Introduction

The Adirondack Park is a hiker's nirvana. While known as a mountainous area, the Adirondacks also boast a myriad of paths to lakes and ponds, waterfalls, and rivers. At over 6 million acres, this state park is larger than Yellowstone, Yosemite, and Glacier National Parks combined. Though a patchwork of public land (48 percent) and private land (52 percent), most of the hiking trails lie within the designated wilderness or wild forests. The twenty-five hikes in this book are spread throughout the Adirondacks. No matter where you are in the park, you'll find the best easy ones nearby.

And as for mountaintops, forty-six of them in the Adirondack Park are over 4,000 feet tall. Becoming an "Adirondack 46er" requires bagging all of these peaks. It's a challenging quest, as twenty of the peaks are extremely remote, even by Adirondack standards, and trail-less, though unofficial "herd paths" now lead to all of the trail-less summits. But there is one that qualifies as a "best easy day hike"—Cascade Mountain, which is described in this book.

Of course, rating a hike "best" and "easiest" is subjective, though not haphazard. The routes in this book are generally under 6 miles long and promise a big reward for relatively modest effort. You'll find eye-popping views, as well as water, wildlife, unique geologic formations, and interesting plant life. I discovered these routes while working on the three editions of my larger book, *Hiking the Adirondacks* (FalconGuides). For more ambitious hikes, plus much more information on and photos of the Adirondack Park, consider adding *Hiking the Adirondacks* to your guidebook collection. In the meantime, this book cherry-picks the best easy routes in the park. Enjoy the trails!

Seasons and Weather

The Adirondack Park has four distinct seasons, though they are not evenly spaced throughout the year. During the short summer—July and August—temperatures can hit the 90s on occasion, but the average temperature is a hiker-friendly 68 degrees Fahrenheit. It's also perfect bug-hatching weather. The black flies can be relentless from early June through mid-July, then the mosquitoes take over, especially around streams, beaver ponds, and lakeshores. Don't leave the car without bug repellent.

Fall comes quickly after Labor Day with the first frost. It's a favorite season for hiking due to the vibrant foliage and lack of bugs. The leaves change first in the High Peaks and northern Adirondacks. Peak color in these two regions usually occurs during the last week of September. Other parts of the park hold their color a week or two longer. Expect ice on the northern side of the taller mountains and be prepared for snow at any time after the first week in October.

Most of the hikes in this book make excellent winter hikes and snowshoeing routes, though not for the inexperienced. Adirondack winters are harsh, with snow and ice storms periodically halting wilderness travel. It's among the coldest places in the Lower 48, with temperatures dipping as low as minus-40 degrees Fahrenheit. If you plan a winter hike, be prepared with the right clothing, footwear, snowshoes, crampons, and ski poles. Check the weather and avalanche conditions before venturing into the backcountry, particularly in the High Peaks region above tree line.

Mud season—April and May—is the only time of the year to avoid hiking in the Adirondacks. Snow can linger on the mountains and in sheltered valleys. Stay off the trails during mud season for the trails' sake. Many routes climb directly up slopes rather than around switchbacks, making them more susceptible to erosion from foot traffic when conditions are muddy.

Discrepancies with Distance

Distances in this book vary from what you might see on trail signs for several reasons. Some trail signs are old and not accurate due to various rerouted sections over time or simply because of the way many trails were measured during the mid to late 1900s, using a surveyor's wheel. Each trail in this book has been measured by a Garmin GPS at least twice. In general, a GPS device is more accurate than a cell phone app, which many hikers now use to track their progress. Don't sweat one or two tenths of a mile. To ensure that you don't commit to a hike that might be too long for your ability level, distances are conservative, meaning if there is a discrepancy among the various ways to measure a trail, the stated mileage errs on the longer side.

Elevation gain is also listed for each hiked based on two GPS readings, which take into account all of the ups and downs of a route, rather than just the elevations at the trailhead and the summit.

Backcountry Checklist

Regardless of the time of year, whenever you head into the Adirondacks, you should expect to encounter high humidity and the chance of precipitation. Waterproof-breathable footwear, wool or wool-blend socks, and quick-drying, non-cotton apparel are de rigueur. In addition, here's a list of essential items to put in your backpack. This is a fair-weather list. Winter hikers will need additional items:

- Bug repellent
- Rain gear
- Fleece or wool sweater
- Wool hat
- Ball cap
- Sunscreen
- Food
- Water (all trailside water sources carry risk of giardia)
- This book! (or a trail map)
- GPS or cell phone with navigation app
- Compass
- First-aid kit
- Whistle
- Waterproof matches or a reliable lighter
- Flashlight or headlamp
- Swiss Army knife or other multi-tool
- Bandana
- Watch

Trail Contacts

In case of emergency, dial 911. ***Note:*** Mobile phone service in the Adirondacks outside of major towns is unreliable.

Adirondack Mountain Club (ADK): Member Services: PO Box 4390, 959 Route 9, Queensbury, NY 12804; (518)

668-4447. Cascade Welcome Center: 4833 Cascade Road, Lake Placid, NY 12946; (518) 837-5047. Heart Lake Program Center: PO Box 867, 1002 Adirondack Loj Road, Lake Placid, NY 12946; (518) 523-3441; www.adk.org

Adirondack Mountain Reserve (Ausable Club), 32 Lake Road, Keene Valley, NY 12943; www.hikeamr.org

Adirondack Trail Improvement Society (ATIS), PO Box 565, Keene Valley, NY 12943; (518) 576-9157 (ATIS Hut—summer season only); (518) 946-7322 (executive director); www.atistrail.org

New York State Department of Environmental Conservation (NYSDEC): Public Outreach, 625 Broadway, Albany, NY 12233; (518) 402-8044. Region 5 (Adirondack Park–East), 1115 Route 86, PO Box 296, Ray Brook, NY 12977; (518) 897-1200. Region 6 (Adirondack Park–West), 317 Washington Street, Watertown, NY 13601; (315) 785-2239; www.dec.ny.gov

Leave No Trace

The Adirondack Park is a big place, but if every visitor to its pristine backcountry left only a small mark, it would quickly be destroyed. As at home, do not litter—not even biodegradables such as orange peels. While they may degrade over time, it takes longer than you think, and they are not part of the park's natural ecosystem. At the same time, take only pictures. Picking a flower may seem harmless, but it could be an endangered species. Likewise, leave wildlife alone both for your safety and their survival.

While it is impossible to have zero impact as you pass through the Adirondack Park, here are some key ways to minimize evidence of your visit:

1. Leave with everything you brought in.
2. Leave no sign of your visit.
3. Leave the landscape as you found it.
4. Pack out or bury human and pet poop.

One easy way to be a low-impact hiker is to simply stay on the trail. Walking around mud holes may keep your boots drier and cleaner, but it widens the trail over time. In addition, avoid taking shortcuts and cutting corners on switchbacks. It may save a few seconds here and there, but it increases erosion and leaves unsightly scars in the woods. Above tree line it is vital that you stay on the trail, walking on rock as much as possible. Fragile alpine plants grow very slowly, enduring the harsh mountaintop environment, but they cannot withstand trampling.

Finally, control your pet and be considerate of others. Voices carry, particularly across bodies of water. Try to keep noise to a minimum so that all can enjoy the serenity of the wilderness.

For more information, visit www. LNT.org.

Trail Finder

Best Hikes for Small Children
6. Mount Jo Loop
10. Mount Arab
11. Goodman Mountain
21. Bald Mountain (Rondaxe)

Best Hikes for Dogs
1. Baxter Mountain
5. Jay Mountain
13. Saint Regis Mountain
17. Moxham Mountain

Best Hikes to Views of the High Peaks
2. The Brothers
3. Cascade Mountain
4. Giant's Nubble via the Ridge Trail
7. Noonmark Mountain
9. Rooster Comb

Best Hikes to Bald Spots
2. The Brothers
3. Cascade Mountain
4. Giant's Nubble via the Ridge Trail
5. Jay Mountain
7. Noonmark Mountain
8. Balancing Rocks (Pitchoff Mountain)
11. Goodman Mountain
13. Saint Regis Mountain
15. Castle Rock Loop
17. Moxham Mountain
21. Bald Mountain (Rondaxe)

| 22. | Black Bear Mountain |
| 23. | Buck Mountain |

Best Wildflower Hikes

10.	Mount Arab
12.	Lyon Mountain
22.	Black Bear Mountain

Best Hikes to Fire Towers

10.	Mount Arab
12.	Lyon Mountain
13.	Saint Regis Mountain
14.	Blue Mountain
16.	Goodnow Mountain
19.	Hadley Mountain
20.	Kane Mountain Loop
21.	Bald Mountain (Rondaxe)
24.	Poke-O-Moonshine Mountain

Best Hikes for Water Lovers

4.	Giant's Nubble via the Ridge Trail
13.	Saint Regis Mountain
18.	Crane Mountain–Crane Pond Loop
25.	Shelving Rock Falls and Lake George

Best Fall Foliage Hikes

1.	Baxter Mountain
9.	Rooster Comb
13.	Saint Regis Mountain
17.	Moxham Mountain
22.	Black Bear Mountain
24.	Poke-O-Moonshine Mountain

Map Legend

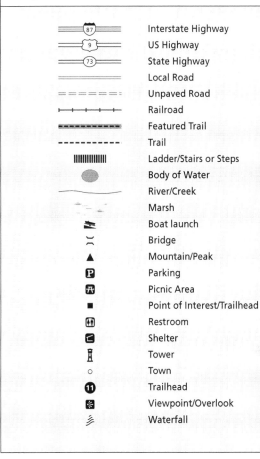

87	Interstate Highway
9	US Highway
73	State Highway
	Local Road
======	Unpaved Road
+—+—+—+	Railroad
▬▬▬▬	Featured Trail
- - - - -	Trail
‖‖‖‖‖	Ladder/Stairs or Steps
⬭	Body of Water
⌒	River/Creek
	Marsh
⬌	Boat launch
⏝	Bridge
▲	Mountain/Peak
🅿	Parking
🛉	Picnic Area
■	Point of Interest/Trailhead
🚻	Restroom
⬟	Shelter
🗼	Tower
○	Town
⑪	Trailhead
◐	Viewpoint/Overlook
〰	Waterfall

While the High Peaks region of the Adirondacks is best known for its forty-six peaks over 4,000 feet in elevation, it also boasts numerous hikes with equally stunning views that don't reach that lauded benchmark. In this section, you'll find Cascade Mountain, considered the easiest of the 4,000-footers, as well as a number of other hikes more modest in terms of summit elevation, but superlative in enjoyment. With big rewards for less effort, these routes are perfect for a family outing, but don't expect solitude, as they attract many school groups and summer camps. Always be prepared with proper footwear, clothing, food, water, and emergency items when attempting any hikes in the High Peaks, no matter how easy they may sound. This area always has a high chance of extreme weather, twelve months of the year.

1 Baxter Mountain

A local favorite to a nice view of many landmark mountains in the High Peaks region.

Total distance: 2.8 miles
Type of hike: Out and back
Highest point: 2,341 feet
Vertical gain: 741 feet

Hiking time: About 2.5 hours
Canine compatibility: Yes. This is a great puppy hike!
Map: USGS Keene Valley Quad

Finding the trailhead: From the junction of NY 73 and NY 9N, go 2 miles on NY 9N east up a steep hill toward Elizabethtown. The trailhead is on your right, across from Hurricane Road. **Trailhead GPS:** N44 13.253' / W73 44.971'

The Hike

There are three approaches up Baxter Mountain. This one (blue NYSDEC markers) is the shortest and easiest. The trail is smooth and flat as you enter the woods. It immediately passes through a power-line cut and then climbs easily through white birch, hemlock, and firs.

At 0.2 miles, it ascends some broad log steps as more hardwoods come into the mix, and then becomes steeper, though nothing harsh.

At 0.4 miles, the trail flattens briefly, then bends sharply to the right (west). For the next half-mile, the ascent is aided by a series of elongated switchbacks. The footing is easy, relatively clear of rocks and roots.

At 0.9 miles, you'll climb over a brief hump that's stabilized by rocks and roots, shortly before coming to the junction with the Beede Road Trail (yellow markers). Bear right, continuing uphill following the blue markers.

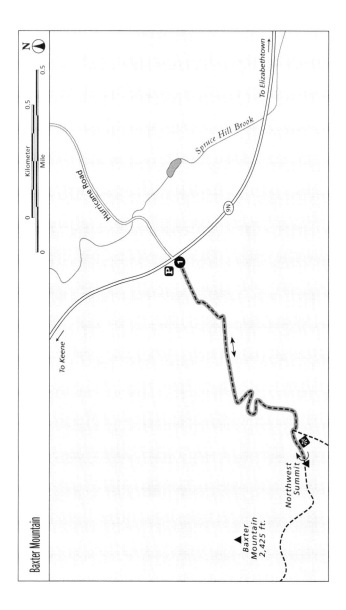

The trail becomes steeper, with more roots and slab. At 1 mile, a lookout is on your left with a view toward Giant Mountain which pokes above some nearby hills. Wild blueberries grow around the opening. Just beyond this first viewpoint, you'll climb past a sign marking a state wild forest boundary.

At 1.2 miles, the trail breaks free of the canopy at a bigger rocky perch laden with more wild blueberries, then dips for a short way. When it turns uphill again, you cross more slab to another open rocky spot and still more blueberries.

At 1.3 miles, you'll reach yet another ledgy lookout. From here, bear right (north), continuing uphill in the woods, not across the ledges.

At 1.4 miles, the summit, a boulder in the trees with a small cairn on top, is visible on your left. Go just a few steps farther to another wonderful open ledge.

Giant Mountain dominates the panorama to the south. Nippletop and a number of the other High Peaks lie to the southwest. Hurricane Mountain is to the east, easily identified by its fire tower.

Return to the trailhead by the same route.

Miles and Directions

0.0   Start at the trailhead on the side of NY 9N.

0.2   Ascend log steps.

0.4   Begin a series of elongated switchbacks.

0.9   Bear right at the junction with Beede Road Trail, following the blue trail markers.

1.0   First viewpoint on your left.

1.2   Enjoy a second view and the blueberries from a rocky perch.

1.3   Another ledgy lookout. Continue uphill to the right in the woods.

1.4   Summit. Return by the same route.

2.8   Arrive back at the trailhead.

2 **The Brothers**

An Adirondack classic to a series of three rock ledges on the shoulder of Big Slide Mountain that rewards with multiple views and acres of wild blueberries.

Total distance: 5.2 miles
Type of hike: Out and back
Highest point: 3,681 feet
Vertical gain: 2,157 feet

Hiking time: About 5 hours
Canine compatibility: Dog-friendly
Map: USGS Keene Valley Quad

Finding the trailhead: From NY 73 in Keene Valley, turn right (west) on Adirondack Street. The road narrows and becomes Johns Brook Lane then turns to dirt. After 1.5 miles from the turn onto Adirondack Street, the road ends at the trailhead called The Garden. If the parking lot is full, there is an overflow lot at Marcy Field, north of Keene Valley on NY 73, with a hiker shuttle to The Garden. The shuttle typically runs only on weekends and holidays during the summer. **Trailhead GPS:** N44 11.224' / W73 48.875'

The Hike

The hike to The Brothers, a series of three ledges laden with blueberries and impressive views, is part of the more epic 10-miler to the summit of Big Slide (4,199 feet). Some maps show The Brothers as a separate peak, but it is really a shoulder of massive Big Slide. *Note:* If you decide to continue to Big Slide, the climb above The Brothers to the summit of Big Slide is not dog-friendly due to ladders and steep rock chimneys.

Each Brother is a lovely destination in itself, so you can decide how far you want to go based on how you feel at that moment and the weather. First Brother and Second Brother reward with superb views. Third Brother, the highest point described here, has a wooded summit except for a good view of the summit of Big Slide.

From the trailhead, take the right trail (blue NYSDEC markers). It's a steady climb from the start. The footing is good at first, with only some roots crisscrossing the trail through a forest dominated by maple and paper birch.

At 0.3 miles, an old trail to Porter Mountain, now closed, departs to the right. Continue straight, climbing the first of the three Brothers. The trail ascends moderately to a height of land, then dips down over a streamlet, which might be dry. From here, the climb continues, soon becoming persistent and rocky underfoot.

The forest is airy and speckled with glacial erratics (boulders). The trail passes between a couple of these impressive boulders to a yellow arrow, pointing left, at 0.7 miles. Two short switchbacks take you around one of the giant rocks, then up a steep section. As the path curls up through more rocks, watch for more yellow arrows painted on the rocks to avoid false detours.

At 0.9 miles, the route bends right around a hump of slab, passing a clearing on your left. Just ahead, you come to an open rock knob and the first view of the Great Range. After this lookout, the path is level, then up, then level again as you parallel the cliff edge but in the woods. When you come to a rock chimney, bear right at its base (not up it), then dip deeper into the woods following a low rock wall, an extension of the chimney. When the rock wall peters out, the path swings left climbing above it. Look back to see a view of the fire tower on Hurricane Mountain.

The route continues paralleling the cliffs, sometimes in the woods and sometimes on open rock. The views of the Great Range get better and better as you climb. By 1.3 miles, you crest First Brother. The view includes, from left to right,

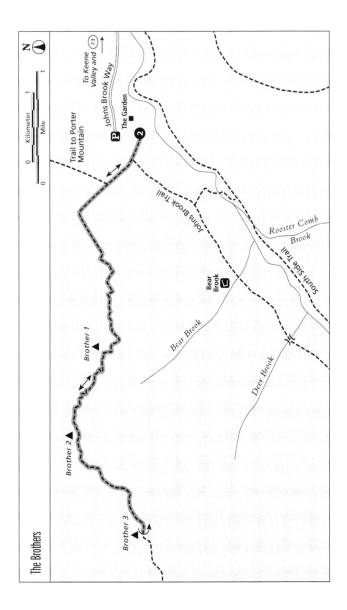

The Brothers

N

Kilometer
0   1

Mile
0   1

Trail to Porter Mountain

To Keene Valley and (73)

Johns Brook Way

The Garden

P

2

Johns Brook Trail

Rooster Comb Brook

South Side Trail

Bear Brook

Bear Brook

Brother 1

Brother 2

Brother 3

Deer Brook

Hurricane Mountain, Giant Mountain, the Great Range, and a number of other 4,000-footers deeper into the High Peaks Wilderness. The view is eye-popping and just gets better as you go higher. Wild blueberries are everywhere in early August. It's tempting to pick a ledge, eat blueberries, and forget about the rest of the hike, but you're just getting started!

The trail levels off briefly as you swing back into the woods. Then, it climbs up some rocky rubble to the base of a rock chimney, then up giant rock steps and an extensive stretch of slab to a lookout at 1.6 miles. Now the view includes more peaks west of Hurricane.

By Second Brother the view is almost 360 degrees, off both sides of this long ledgy ridge. You can also see Mount Mansfield, the highest peak in Vermont through a notch in the closer mountains. *Note:* Although the painted blazes on the rocks are yellow, the NYSDEC markers remain blue.

The trail continues through a small depression and then reaches Third Brother at 2.6 miles.

Return by the same route.

Miles and Directions

0.0 Start at The Garden. Take the right trail toward The Brothers (blue NYSDEC markers).

0.3 Continue straight at the junction with the former trail to Porter Mountain.

0.9 Come to a rock knob and the first clear view of The Great Range.

1.3 First Brother. Continue through the woods toward Second Brother.

1.6 Pass a viewpoint on the ledgy ridge with the first view toward Hurricane Mountain.

1.8 Second Brother. Continue toward Third Brother.

2.6 Third Brother. Return by the same route.

5.2 Arrive back at The Garden.

3 Cascade Mountain

The easiest of the Adirondack 4,000-footers and a great "starter" hike, with views of numerous other Adirondack peaks, Lake Champlain, and the Green Mountains of Vermont.

Total distance: 4.8 miles
Type of hike: Out and back
Highest point: 4,098 feet
Vertical gain: 1,883 feet

Hiking time: About 4.5 hours
Canine compatibility: Dog-friendly. Dogs must be on leash.
Map: USGS Keene Valley Quad

Finding the trailhead: From the junction of NY 73 and Old Military Road by the fairgrounds and the Olympic ski jump complex in Lake Placid, follow NY 73 east for 6 miles. The trailhead is on the right (south) side of the road just before Upper Cascade Lake. From the junction of NY 73 and 9N in Keene, follow NY 73 toward Lake Placid for 6.6 miles. **Trailhead GPS:** N44 13.136' / W73 53.254'

The Hike

Cascade Mountain is a popular hike, so it's best to get an early start if you want a parking spot in one of the turnouts by the trailhead. This is a good one for older kids and for less-experienced hikers looking for a big reward without serious mileage. It's also the perfect hike for the road-weary looking for some exercise after a long drive into the Adirondack Park but without a big time commitment—plus you get credit for bagging a 4,000-footer.

Note: Though Cascade Mountain is considered entry-level by seasoned hikers, it is still a 4,000-footer, with an exposed summit. Expect wind, and be prepared for cold temperatures and sudden weather changes even on a fair summer day. There is a lot of open rock, which can be slick when wet. Save this one for a nice day.

From the trailhead, descend a log-framed staircase, then cross four short lengths of puncheon to the sign-in box. This well-used trail follows red NYSDEC markers, ascending immediately from the box. There are lots of rocks and roots on the eroded, heavily traveled trail. Water bars and well-placed stones help keep this popular trail in shape.

The wide trail climbs at a comfortable rate, heading south through a mixed northern forest of birch, striped maple, and beech. There are breaks in the ascent, first to cross a stream on a footbridge at 0.3 miles that flows down a pretty, mossy cascade just above the trail, and second to pass through a mud hole on large stepping stones. From the mud hole, the path heads deeper into the forest to the southeast. Soon it begins to climb steadily again and becomes rockier.

At 0.9 miles, the trail mellows, though it remains cobbled. By 1.2 miles the forest changes. Hemlock and birch signal your approach to the lower boreal zone, though a few maples remain in the mix. More slab appears under foot, and you start to feel higher on the mountain.

At 1.5 miles, the trail zigs right then zags left, like "S" turns, though the curves are not really switchbacks that aid the ascent on this high buttress of the mountain. There isn't much of a view yet, though you can sense an expanse and mountains on your left.

The trail eases as it winds through the woods, passing over a couple of short puncheon steps. At 1.8 miles, you scramble up several short rock walls, only a couple feet tall with one shaped like natural steps.

The slabby route traverses among spindly conifers covered with lichen and dripping with Spanish moss. At 2 miles, a more substantial rock chimney blocks the trail, though it's easy to climb up its left side. Just beyond lies an open rock perch with the first real view. From here you can see the Olympic ski jumps and the village of Lake Placid to the north, nearly swallowed up by acre after acre of hills and forest. Mount Marcy looms large to the west.

The trail reenters the trees, continuing to the northeast over more slab and mud, with puncheon helping to keep your boots dry at least part of the way. At 2.1 miles, the trail comes to a three-way junction at a broad, flat rock. The right fork goes to Porter Mountain. The left path leads to a privy. Continue straight, following the red markers and the sign to Cascade Mountain.

The trail becomes fairly level, soon passing through a small, grassy, subalpine bog. The trees end just ahead. Follow the yellow painted blazes and rock cairns up the expansive bedrock toward the summit. It's steep, requiring some scrambling and some easy friction climbing in places.

At 2.3 miles, a ladder on the right side of a particularly steep section of bedrock aids the ascent. Above the ladder, the route bears left, continuing up the middle of the open rock. After the top of the next hump, it veers along the right side of a flat spot, following a line of small rocks, placed there to keep foot traffic off the fragile alpine flora.

The trail ends at the summit at 2.4 miles, a broad, long ridge with many places to enjoy the view and have a picnic even if there are lots of people. You can see the fire tower on Hurricane Mountain to the east, Memorial Highway snaking up Whiteface to the north, Lake Placid village and lake to the northwest, and a mesmerizing number of 4,000-footers to the south including the famous Great Range (Gothics, Armstrong, Upper Wolfjaw, and Lower Wolfjaw).

Return to the trailhead by the same route.

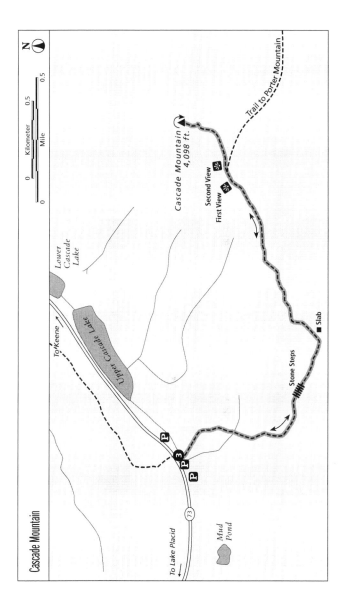

Cascade Mountain

Miles and Directions

0.0 Start at the trailhead. Descend the log-framed stairs into the woods and cross four short lengths of puncheon.

0.3 Cross a stream with a pretty cascade to your left.

1.2 Reach the lower boreal forest and begin to feel your elevation gain.

2.0 View. Climb a rock chimney to a rock perch.

2.1 Continue straight at the three-way junction, then reach tree line.

2.3 Climb a ladder up a particularly steep section of bedrock.

2.4 Summit. Return by the same route.

4.8 Arrive back at the trailhead.

4 Giant's Nubble via the Ridge Trail

A pleasant hike to a remote tarn and a rocky lookout on Giant Mountain, great for those who want a view but don't want to scale an entire 4,000-footer.

Total distance: 4.2 miles
Type of hike: Out and back
Highest point: 2,772 feet
Vertical gain: 1,122 feet

Hiking time: About 3.5 hours
Canine compatibility: Dog-friendly
Map: USGS Keene Valley Quad

Finding the trailhead: From the junction of NY 73 and Ausable Road (the road to the Ausable Club) in St. Huberts, head south on NY 73 for 2.1 miles, past the second entrance to Ausable Road and the parking area for the Roaring Brook Trail. The trailhead for the Ridge Trail is just past Chapel Pond on the left (north) side of the road. There is parking on both sides of the road. Overflow parking is at Marcy Field where a seasonal hiker shuttle, weekends and holidays only, can drop you off at the trailhead. If approaching from I-87, take exit 30, then follow NY 73 and US 9 north for 2.1 miles. Where NY 73 and US 9 split, continue on NY 73 for another 3 miles. **Trailhead GPS:** N44 08.318' / W73 44.597'

The Hike

Giant's Nubble is a knob of rock on the southern side of Giant Mountain, the tallest peak in the Giant Mountain Wilderness. There are two approaches to the Nubble, one via the Roaring Brook Trail and the other via the Ridge Trail, which are 1.3 miles apart on NY 73. If you have two cars, you can start at one end and hike to the other, a 3.2-mile hike. With a car drop, you pass by Giant Washbowl, a serene mountain tarn and the largest body of water in the Giant Mountain

Wilderness, climb to a nice view from atop the Nubble, and have the added bonus of an impressive waterfall near the bottom of the Roaring Brook Trail. The route described here is out-and-back via the Ridge Trail. You'll see the Washbowl and the Nubble, but not the waterfall. ***Note:*** It is not safe to walk between the two trailheads along NY 73, which winds through a narrow ravine, with a guardrail on one side and a steep hillside on the other. The hiker shuttle stops at the two trailheads when it's operating (typically weekends and holidays in July, August, and September).

From the trailhead, the path follows blue NYSDEC markers east into the woods over three short puncheon to the sign-in box. From there, the trail climbs moderately through a hardwood forest typical of the Adirondacks at lower elevations. In early July wild raspberries bloom profusely along the trail.

The path bends left over an intermittent streamlet and then angles to the northeast following the streambed. Though the trail is strewn with rocks and roots, the footing is generally good, with patches of wood sorrel brightening the ground here and there.

At 0.3 miles, you cross a stream and then go up some stone and log steps.

At 0.5 miles, watch for an arrow on a tree atop a boulder, pointing to the right to a stream crossing which is not much more than a rock field in the summer. From there, the route angles upward to the northeast. Another arrow points left as the trail winds up several switchbacks on a steep slope. More steps and other examples of good trail work aid your ascent.

The trail comes alongside a seasonal creek, follows it up another steep rocky pitch, then crosses it. About a half-mile later, you come to a lovely lookout on a rock perch. Chapel Pond lies below, and the Great Range (Gothics, Armstrong, Upper Wolfjaw, and Lower Wolfjaw Mountains) fills the view

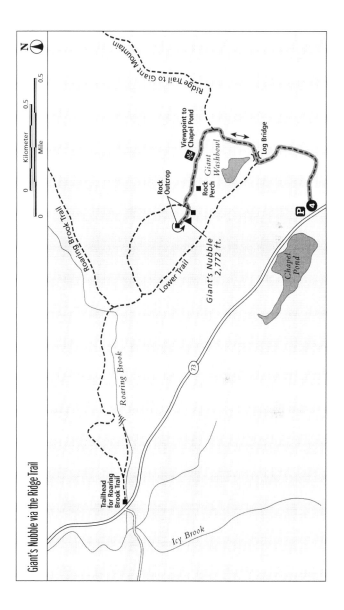

Giant's Nubble via the Ridge Trail

N

Kilometer
0   0.5
Mile
0   0.5

Roaring Brook Trail

Trailhead for Roaring Brook Trail

Roaring Brook

Icy Brook

73

Lower Trail

Giant's Nubble
2,772 ft.

Rock Outcrop

Rock Perch

Giant Washbowl

Viewpoint to Chapel Pond

Ridge Trail to Giant Mountain

Log Bridge

P 4

Chapel Pond

to the southwest. From there, the route continues along a cliff edge, though trees obscure the view until you reach the next section of clear slab.

The grade eases, then at 1.2 miles, the trail dips to a junction with the lower trail to Giant's Nubble. Go right, over a footbridge at one end of Giant Washbowl. Nestled below a cliff, the Washbowl is a 4.2-acre pond that the state stocks with brook trout. It's a pleasant place to take a break.

Continue uphill past a couple of primitive tent sites, then at 1.6 miles, turn left at the upper trail to the Nubble. The path climbs steadily, gaining about 300 feet in about a half mile. At 2.1 miles, you come to the junction with the trail to Roaring Brook Falls. Go left, following the arrow to "Nubble" up one more hump, and you're there.

The Nubble is not a mountaintop, but a prominent knob on the side of Giant Mountain with some lovely views from open slab. From the Nubble, Chapel Pond lies directly below you. Round Mountain is immediately across NY 73, forming the opposite side of the valley, with Noonmark just behind, but the eye is drawn to the Great Range, the string of 4,000-footers just to the right (northwest).

Return to the trailhead by the same route.

Miles and Directions

- **0.0** Start at the trailhead for the Ridge Trail up Giant Mountain.
- **0.3** Cross a stream then ascend stone and rock steps.
- **0.5** Cross a seasonal stream and ascend a rock field (washout).
- **1.0** View. Pass over a rock perch with a view of Chapel Pond and the Great Range.
- **1.2** Giant Washbowl. Continue on the Ridge Trail.
- **2.1** Giant's Nubble. Return by the same route.
- **4.2** Arrive back at the trailhead.

5 Jay Mountain

The only trail in the Jay Mountain Wilderness, it takes you to a stunning panorama of the High Peaks from Giant Mountain to Whiteface Mountain.

Total distance: 5.4 miles
Type of hike: Out and back
Highest point: 3,600 feet
Vertical gain: 2,200 feet

Hiking time: About 5 hours
Canine compatibility: Dog-friendly
Map: USGS Jay Mountain Quad

Finding the trailhead: From NY 9N in Upper Jay, just south of the bridge over the East Branch of the Ausable River, turn east on Trumbulls Road (Essex CR 85). Go 3.3 miles to the hiker parking lot across from the intersection with Upland Meadows Road. *Note:* At 2.9 miles, Trumbulls Road becomes Jay Mountain Road after the junction with Anthony Road. **Trailhead GPS:** N44 18.574' / W73 43.145'

The Hike

Jay Mountain is really two peaks, east and west, connected by Grassy Notch, the saddle between the two summits. With its twin tops, Jay Mountain is often called simply "The Jays" by local hikers. The east summit is higher, though the maintained section of trail only goes to the west summit. This hiking description covers the route to the west summit.

The Jays was a sleeper hike until 2010, when the NYS-DEC finalized its plan for the Jay Mountain Wilderness. The plan included turning the unofficial herd path to the west summit into an official trail. It is the only NYSDEC-maintained hiking trail in the Jay Mountain Wilderness, the smallest wilderness area in the Adirondack Park at 7,951 acres.

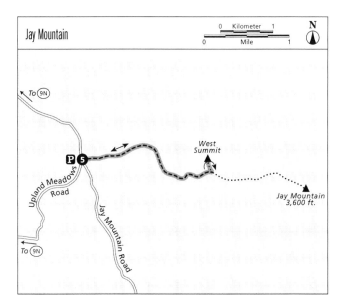

The trail to the west peak ascends at a reasonable grade, with good footing. During the spring, a plethora of wildflowers bloom along the lower trail, including clintonia, trillium, spring beauties, white baneberry, Dutchman's britches, and yellow violets.

As you enter the woods, the remains of an old stone wall are on your left before the sign-in box. Another one lies to your right just after that. These stone walls harken back to a period in the 1800s when this spot was a farm. The forest has now reclaimed the land. They are common when hiking in New England but less so in the Adirondacks, where the rugged terrain was more conducive to hunting and trapping than farming.

The ascent is steady from the start and only lets up at 1.4 miles, when the trail dips to a seasonal stream.

At 2.3 miles, you can catch glimpses into the High Peaks of Mount Marcy and the Great Range through the trees which are thin and are dominated by hemlocks more than hardwoods.

At 2.7 miles, a short spur on your left leads to the west summit and a stunning panorama of the High Peaks from Giant Mountain to Whiteface Mountain. You can also see along the undulating ledgy ridge leading to the east summit. In early August, acres of wild blues carpet this memorable viewpoint.

Return by the same route.

Miles and Directions

0.0 Start at the trailhead on Jay Mountain Road by the junction with Upland Meadows Road.

1.4 Dip to a seasonal stream.

2.7 West summit. Return by the same route.

5.4 Arrive back at the trailhead.

6 Mount Jo Loop

A short, kid-friendly hike along an interpretive trail to a big view of the High Peaks.

Total distance: 2.6 miles
Type of hike: Loop
Highest point: 2,876 feet
Vertical gain: 708 feet

Hiking time: About 2 hours
Canine compatibility: Dog-friendly. Dogs should be on leash.
Map: USGS North Elba Quad

Finding the trailhead: From Lake Placid, take NY 73 east toward Keene. Go 1.5 miles past the entrance to the Olympic ski jump complex. Turn right (south) on Adirondack Loj Road. Go 4.6 miles to the end of the road and the hiker parking area at Adirondak Loj. *Note:* Fee for parking, discounted for members of the Adirondack Mountain Club. **Trailhead GPS:** N44 11.094' / W73 57.810'

The Hike

Mount Jo is a small hike that delivers a close-in look at many of the tallest mountains in the Adirondacks. Its trailhead shares a parking lot with the trailheads to Mount Marcy, Algonquin Peak, Wright Peak, and a number of the other giants.

Originally called Bear Mountain, it was renamed in the 1870s for Josephine Schofield, fiancée of Henry Van Hoevenberg, the Adirondack guide who masterminded the original Adirondak Loj and who laid out many of the trails that begin here. Schofield and Van Hoevenberg were engaged after camping with a group of friends by Upper Ausable Lake during the summer of 1877. Schofield's parents were adamantly opposed to the engagement. She died mysteriously before the marriage, and the heartbroken Van Hoevenberg named Mount Jo in her memory while building the home beside Heart Lake that they had planned to build together. However, instead of a modest home, he built an enormous log lodge, the original Adirondak Loj, considered the largest free-standing log structure in the country at the time.

In 1903, a forest fire burned the lodge and most of the surrounding forest. As with other bald peaks in the Adirondack Park that are technically below tree line, the summit of Mount Jo remains open because the soil quickly eroded away after the fire cleared the flora at this low but exposed point. Today the trail takes you through mature second-growth forest then ends at a fine viewpoint.

Mount Jo is popular among school groups and summer camps, so expect company at the summit. It follows an interpretive trail. You can buy an inexpensive brochure for the interpretive trail at the nature museum, a small cabin near the edge of Heart Lake, a short way into the hike. There are two approaches to the summit, the Long Trail and the Short Trail, which combined make a nice loop as described here.

The trail as measured in this description starts at the edge of the hiker parking lot near the ADK High Peaks Information Center. Follow a footpath covered with wood chips toward the parking toll booth. Cross the road at the toll booth, and continue on the manicured gravel path, following the sign to Mount Jo and the orange ADK trail markers.

After passing several buildings tucked into the trees on the Adirondak Loj campus, at 0.2 miles, you come to a T near the edge of Heart Lake, which is ahead of you through the trees. Turn right (northwest), passing the nature museum. In another 100 feet the trail to Rocky Falls and Indian Pass departs to the left. Turn right again, heading away from Heart Lake. A few steps later, you cross a two-log footbridge and come to the sign-in box.

Beyond the box, the well-maintained trail ascends steadily over rocks and roots, intermittent waterbars, and stone steps. This is the nature trail, with numbered signposts along the way. At 0.5 miles, the trail splits. The Long Trail departs to the left. Take the Short Trail to the right. You will close the loop here later.

The Short Trail turns uphill up stone steps and a lot more rocks, heading north. It soon flattens across a muddy area. Many stepping stones help keep your feet dry. The trail crosses a streamlet several times then swings around a mammoth boulder with a birch tree on top. The tree's roots snake 20 feet down the rock into the soil beside the trail. From here, the climb becomes more persistent up more rocks that pave the trail like giant cobblestones. As you weave among several more large "glacial erratics" (boulders left behind after the last ice age), the pitch looks even steeper, but many well-positioned rocks make it feel more like an uneven staircase rather than a difficult climb.

Eventually, a rock wall appears beside the trail on your right, which peters out but not the ascent. More stone steps help you continue upward. After climbing a steep rock slab, you reach the upper junction with the Long Trail at 1 mile. Turn right, following the arrow toward the summit. The grade eases as you cross several lengths of puncheon through a potentially muddy area.

At 1.1 miles, three consecutive ladder-like wooden staircases take you up a particularly vertical section of slab. From there, continue up the bedrock where a sign points you toward the summit at 1.2 miles.

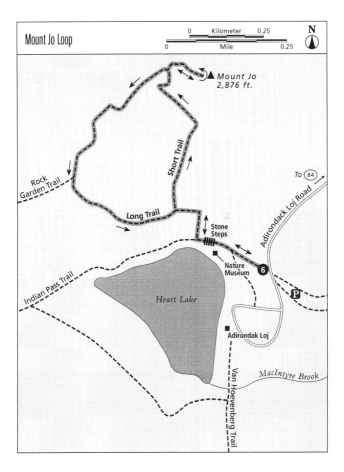

The top of Mount Jo is a rock knob with a spectacular view of the McIntyre Range (mainly Algonquin and Iroquois Peaks) above Heart Lake. There are other viewpoints in other directions as you walk around the summit plateau, though trees have grown up in recent years, obscuring some of the view.

From the summit, retrace back to the upper junction of the Long Trail and the Short Trail at 1.4 miles. This time, go straight (west), following the red trail markers and heading down the steeper route, though it is only steeper than the Short Trail for a short way and much less rocky. The Long Trail is mostly joint-friendly dirt, with some roots across the path. It becomes more rock-strewn and eventually rather eroded like a streambed but only for a short section.

At the bottom of the slope, the trail bends left (south) onto smooth, dry ground, passing under a 25-foot-high rock wall before coming to the junction with the Rock Garden Trail at 1.6 miles. Bear left (south) at the junction, staying on the Long Trail.

The trail passes under another impressive rock outcropping as you continue downhill, sometimes over some slab, as you traverse to the east. The path eventually levels off, crosses a wooden footbridge then closes the loop with the Short Trail at 2.1 miles.

Continue straight (the right fork) and retrace back to the Adirondak Loj campus. Arrive back at the trailhead at 2.6 miles.

Miles and Directions

0.0 Start at the hiker parking lot. Follow the wood-chip path and signs past the parking toll booth onto the Adirondak Loj campus.

0.2 Turn right at the T, passing the nature museum, then in another 100 feet turn right at the junctions with the trail to Rocky Falls and Indian Pass.

0.5 Turn right on the Short Trail at the lower junction with the Long Trail.

1.0 Bear right at the upper junction with the Long Trail.

1.1 Climb three ladder-like staircases.

1.2 Summit. Retrace back to the upper junction with the Long Trail.

1.4 Go straight at the upper junction with the Long Trail, following the Long Trail downhill.

1.6 Bear left at the junction with the Rock Garden Trail, continuing on the Long Trail.

2.1 Close the loop at the lower junction with the Short Trail.

2.6 Arrive back at the trailhead.

7 Noonmark Mountain

A steady climb to a summit ledge with many views of the 4,000-footers, including the iconic Great Range, not only from the top but also from the open rock along much of the upper route.

Total distance: 6 miles
Type of hike: Out and back
Highest point: 3,471 feet
Vertical gain: 2,280 feet
Hiking time: About 5.5 hours

Canine compatibility: No. Dogs are not allowed on Ausable Club and Adirondack Mountain Reserve lands.
Map: USGS Keene Valley Quad

Finding the trailhead: From the bridge over Johns Brook in Keene Valley, travel 3.3 miles east on NY 73 to St. Huberts. At the second junction with Ausable Road, turn right. Go about 100 yards. The trailhead parking lot is on the left. This is the same parking lot for the hikes to Mount Colvin and the Great Range. Parking is free, but reservations are required in advance through the AMR website, hikeamr.org. Parking is not permitted along Ausable Road. **Trailhead parking GPS:** N44 08.982' / W73 46.078'

The Hike

Noonmark Mountain is so named because it is due south of Keene Valley and marks the noon position of the sun. It's a sturdy 2,280 feet of vertical gain in only 3 miles, but there is a lot to see along the way as you scramble up rocks and ladders.

From the hiker parking lot, continue up Ausable Road on foot. This dirt road is private, one of two ways into the heart of the Ausable Club, but a public right-of-way for hikers.

At 0.3 miles, at the corner of the golf course, the trailhead for the Noonmark Trail, also known as the Stimson Trail, is on your left, concurrent with a dirt road called Noonmark Trail Way. It is named for Henry Stimson who created the route almost a century ago. Turn left onto the Stimson Trail. A sign says "private," however the hiker sign-in box is there as witness to this public right-of-way. Please stay on the road. It seems as if you are walking up a driveway, and you will pass several of them, following the yellow NYSDEC trail markers.

At 0.5 miles, bear right onto a footpath at an arrow pointing the way. The trail climbs a little more, then flattens under tall hemlocks and soon crosses a couple of seasonal streamlets.

At 0.8 miles, the far side of a slightly larger stream marks the boundary between the AMR and the High Peaks Wilderness. After crossing the boundary onto state land, the climb becomes more obvious but is still moderate. A sizable stream (unreliable) lies below you on the left in a small gorge.

At 1 mile, you come to the junction with the Dix Mountain Trail. Bear right, staying on the Stimson Trail, following the red markers. The climb now becomes steep, but it soon moderates as you pass through a classic northern temperate forest. When the trail turns up again, lots of trail work, including many stone steps, aid the ascent. Soon, you reach the first of many sections of vertical rock slab. Bear right to stay on the official trail. Above this point the trail becomes more cobbled up the next pitch, then a few switchbacks give some relief.

At 1.8 miles, a long stone wall parallels the trail, which terraces the hillside and eventually heads up the wall via a break in its even, vertical face. The route zigs left then zags right up the rocks as you start to sense your elevation gain.

At 2.2 miles, you get your first view of the Great Range through a cut in the trees. Hedgehog Mountain is the rounded peak with the big scar. A moment later, there's a beautiful view of Giant Mountain across the gap and many wild blueberries at your feet.

Above this first perch, the trail enters the boreal forest and becomes a patchwork of slab and ledge. The trees thin as you leave the view of Giant Mountain behind. There are more large rocks to scramble up as you ascend a high shoulder of the mountain. From here, the trail continues through the conifers and tons of blueberries.

At 2.5 miles, you come to the first of two ladders, a short one up a half-buried boulder. The ladders are separated by a rock chimney and a view of the Great Range, plus a look at the summit of Noonmark as you climb. The second ladder aids the ascent up a longer rock chimney. Finish the climb up this particularly vertical spot using the steps and crack in the rock.

The route is now more open in the subalpine zone with many lookouts as you scramble up more rock. At 3 miles, the trail meets a 15-foot-high vertical wall. Head right to get on top of it, which is the summit of Noonmark. There is a 360-degree view that includes Giant Mountain to the north, Lake Champlain and the Green Mountains in Vermont to the east, and the Great Range and Mount Marcy to the west and a number of other 4,000-footers.

Return by the same route.

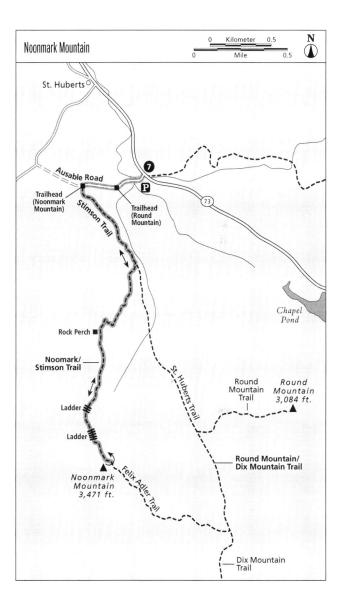

Noonmark Mountain

St. Huberts

Ausable Road

Trailhead (Noonmark Mountain)

Trailhead (Round Mountain)

P

7

73

Stimson Trail

Rock Perch

Noomark/ Stimson Trail

Ladder

Ladder

Noonmark Mountain 3,471 ft.

Felix Adler Trail

St. Huberts Trail

Chapel Pond

Round Mountain Trail

Round Mountain 3,084 ft.

Round Mountain/ Dix Mountain Trail

Dix Mountain Trail

N

0   Kilometer   0.5

0   Mile   0.5

Miles and Directions

0.0 Start at the hiker parking lot on Ausable Road, then walk up Ausable Road (dirt).

0.3 At the corner of the golf course, turn left at the trailhead sign for Noonmark Mountain on the Stimson Trail.

0.5 Bear right at the arrow onto a footpath.

0.8 Cross the boundary into the High Peaks Wilderness on the far side of a seasonal stream.

1.0 Bear right at the junction with the Dix Mountain Trail, continuing on the Stimson Trail.

1.8 Traverse the hillside parallel to a long rock wall, then head up a crack in it.

2.2 View. Pass a view of Giant Mountain through a cut in the trees, then a view of the Great Range from a rock perch.

2.5 Climb the first of two ladders.

3.0 Summit. Return by the same route.

6.0 Arrive back at the hiker parking lot.

8 Balancing Rocks (Pitchoff Mountain)

An invigorating hike to balancing boulders on a broad rock plateau with a view of Mount Marcy and other Adirondack 4,000-footers.

Total distance: 3 miles
Type of hike: Out and back
Highest point: 2,950 feet
Vertical gain: 775 feet

Hiking time: About 2.5 hours
Canine compatibility: Dog-friendly
Map: USGS Keene Valley Quad

Finding the trailhead: From the junction of NY 73 and Old Military Road (by the fairgrounds in Lake Placid), go 6.1 miles on NY 73 to the popular trailhead for Cascade Mountain just above Cascade Lake. *Note:* Arrive early to get a parking spot. Begin at the trailhead for the Sentinel Range Wilderness on the opposite (north) side of the road. **Trailhead GPS:** N44 13.157' / W73 53.218'

The Hike

Balancing Rocks, also called Balanced Rocks, is on a shoulder of Pitchoff Mountain, which lies at the edge of the Sentinel Range Wilderness. It's a lovely hike to a curious group of boulders perched on the edge of a tall cliff. The boulders look as if they should roll to the valley at any second, but they haven't moved since the last ice age receded, 10,000 years ago, and left them where they now stand. It's a perfect first hike with kids due to this geologic curiosity. It's also a good choice if you are pressed for time, but want to get a little exercise and see a nice view.

Following the red NYSDEC markers, the hike leaves the side of NY 73 up a short, steep staircase. From the sign-in box, it's a steep but quick ascent up the hillside on an obvious footpath, then the trail levels off, running northeast, parallel to NY 73.

At 0.8 miles, a short spur on the right takes you to the first lookout, mainly an unobstructed view of Cascade Mountain, with Algonquin Peak poking up to the right.

At 1 mile, you pass by giant boulders, called glacial erratics, on both sides of the trail as the climb gets more decisive. It passes a better view from another lookout, with Mount Colden, Wright Peak, and the tip of Mount Marcy now into the mix. From here the trail is steeper and rougher with several places where you must scramble over large rocks.

At 1.5 miles, you reach a T, which is the junction with the spur to the Balancing Rocks. Turn right, crossing open bedrock toward Cascade Mountain. After passing two rocks that form a tilted chair in the middle of the path, you come to a ledge with one moderate-sized rock on it. Bear right, soon breaking onto a broad stretch of open slab with two enormous boulders (and a number of other large rocks) perched at the edge of the precipice. Beyond the rocks, the view is a spectacular panorama. You can see the fire tower on Hurricane Mountain in the distance to the far left (southeast), the Olympic bobsled run to the far right, and with Cascade, Big Slide, Marcy, Colden, and Algonquin filling most of the view in between. The summit of Pitchoff Mountain is visible above you to the north.

Return by the same route.

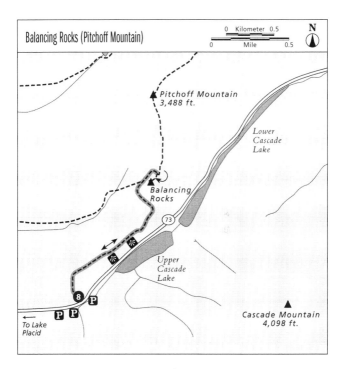

Balancing Rocks (Pitchoff Mountain)

0 Kilometer 0.5
0 Mile 0.5

N

Pitchoff Mountain
3,488 ft.

Lower
Cascade
Lake

Balancing
Rocks

73

Upper
Cascade
Lake

8

P

P   P

← To Lake
Placid

Cascade Mountain
4,098 ft.

Miles and Directions

0.0 Climb the stairs at the trailhead on NY 73 across from the
Cascade Mountain trailhead.

0.8 Take the short spur to the first lookout, mainly of Cascade
Mountain.

1.0 Pass a second viewpoint, this time of Mounts Colden, Wright,
and Marcy.

1.5 Turn right at the T, crossing bedrock to Balancing Rocks.
Retrace your steps back to the trailhead.

3.0 Arrive back at the trailhead.

9 Rooster Comb

This enjoyable hike passes through pleasant woods to a view of Keene Valley, then continues to an exceptional close-in look at the Adirondacks giants.

Total distance: 5.6 miles
Type of hike: Out and back
Highest point: 2,592 feet
Vertical gain: 1,556 feet

Hiking time: About 4.5 hours
Canine compatibility: Dog-friendly
Map: USGS Keene Valley Quad

Finding the trailhead: From the bridge over Johns Brook in Keene Valley, go 0.6 miles on NY 73 east (actually south at this point). The trailhead and substantial parking lot is on the right (west) side of the road at the south end of the village. **Trailhead GPS:** N44 11.124' / W73 47.226'

The Hike

Rooster Comb is a lesser peak compared to its 4,000-foot neighbors, but it offers spectacular closeup views of those neighbors. From the parking area, follow the yellow NYS-DEC markers over a well-constructed footbridge across a boggy backwater. The smooth, obvious trail runs alongside the marsh and then a lovely pond adjacent to a school. This first section of the hike is part of the school's nature trail and a public right-of-way. The woods on your left are private land.

At 0.2 miles, at the junction at the southwest corner of the pond by a half-buried stone foundation, continue straight, heading deeper into the forest and crossing into the High Peaks Wilderness. The trail then begins to climb, aided by stone steps. The ascent is steady under towering hemlocks with little undergrowth. The trees seem like random pillars holding up the sky and provide cool shade on a warm day.

Hardwoods and more undergrowth soon reenter the forest mix as the trail winds up a half-dozen switchbacks. At 0.7 miles, you come to the junction with the trail from Snow Mountain. Bear right (straight), continuing to the southwest and following the yellow markers.

At 1.7 miles, the route crosses a stream, which might be a small trickle after a dry spell, and bends to the right (west). Then it swings left (south) and eases, traversing through maples and beeches, as it continues upward on a moderate grade.

At 2.1 miles, you reach an offset trail junction. The trails to the left go to Hedgehog Mountain, St. Huberts, and the Great Range via Lower Wolfjaw Mountain. Bear right (straight) uphill, following blue NYSDEC markers. The path goes around an enormous glacial erratic, one of many impressive boulders deposited throughout the woods. It dips and traverses to the northeast, passing under a 25-foot rock wall. From here, it climbs some rock steps by another rock outcropping. After a couple of switchbacks, you start to feel the elevation gain as you glimpse a nearby ridge through the trees.

At 2.4 miles, the trail reaches a T. Bear right (northeast) toward Valley View Ledge on a smooth descent, reaching the ledge at 2.5 miles. The view of Keene Valley and Marcy Field is quite pleasing. You can also see the fire tower atop Hurricane Mountain to the east across the valley. The Brothers and the hulk of Big Slide dominate the view to the north.

Retrace your steps back to the main trail at 2.6 miles, then bear right (west), uphill, to continue to Rooster Comb's summit. The final approach to the summit is through classic boreal forest as evidenced by the low spindly conifers and birches. The trail traverses to the south, then bends sharply

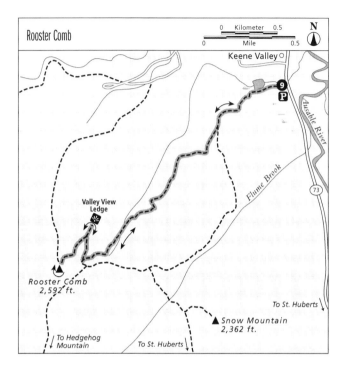

right, up a short but steep bit of slab. It continues to climb more persistently below some ledges, then turns sharply right again up a ladder at 2.8 miles.

After a fun scramble up another ledgy area, you get a great view to the east into Giant Mountain's huge cirque just beyond Round Mountain. NY 73 winds past Chapel Pond along the valley floor like a gray ribbon below you.

After a short, eroded section and several long lengths of slab, you reach the summit of Rooster Comb at 2.9 miles. Head southwest to the open ledge and an awesome view of Giant to the east, Noonmark to the south, and Mount Marcy to the southwest. It's not a 360-degree view, but the close proximity of these big peaks makes up for the partial panorama.

Return by the same route, without the spur to Valley View Ledge.

Miles and Directions

0.0 Start at the hiker parking lot, crossing a footbridge through a marsh.

0.2 Go straight at the southwest corner of the pond and a half-buried stone foundation.

0.7 Bear right (straight) at the junction with the trail to Snow Mountain.

1.7 Cross an unreliable stream.

2.1 Bear right (straight) at the offset junction with trails to Hedgehog Mountain, St. Huberts, and the Great Range.

2.4 Bear right on the spur toward Valley View Ledge.

2.5 Valley View Ledge. Retrace back to the main trail.

2.6 Turn right (uphill), continuing up Rooster Comb.

2.8 Climb a ladder.

2.9 Summit. Return by the same route, but without the spur to Valley View Ledge.

5.6 Arrive back at the trailhead.

The farther you go in the Northern Adirondacks—away from the center of the Adirondack Park—the flatter the land becomes. While the region doesn't have the dramatic topography nor the multitude of bare summits found in other parts of the Adirondack Park, there are still several interesting peaks worth climbing.

Be aware that this is a popular area for hunting bear and deer in the fall. Hunting is permitted on all public land within the Adirondack Park, so it's a good idea to wear hunter-orange if you are hiking here from mid-September through December 31. That said, the biggest hazard to hikers is death by mosquito. Not really, but the insect population thrives on the abundance of water in the region, especially in May and June. Some people wear bug netting, but a ball cap and a coating of bug repellent with at least 30 percent DEET is usually enough to deter the swarm and maintain sanity.

10 Mount Arab

A short, kid-friendly hike to a restored fire tower affording views of lakes and mountains in every direction and a fire-watcher's cabin around which the summer caretaker has created a bird sanctuary.

Total distance: 2.2 miles
Type of hike: Out and back
Highest point: 2,533 feet
Vertical gain: 721 feet
Hiking time: About 2.5 hours

Canine compatibility: Dogs should be on leash. Bring water for your dog. Do not allow your dog on the fire tower.
Map: USGS Piercefield Quad

Finding the trailhead: In Tupper Lake at the junction of NY 3 and NY 30, take NY 3 west for 6.8 miles to Piercefield. Turn left in Piercefield on St. Lawrence CR 62, following the sign to Conifer and Mount Arab (the hamlets). Go 1.7 miles. Turn left on Mount Arab Road. Go 0.8 miles to the trailhead on the left. Trailhead parking is on the right.
Trailhead GPS: N44 12.819' / W74 35.754'

The Hike

Mount Arab is a perfect hike for children and inexperienced hikers. There is a big reward—climbing the fire tower—for relatively little effort. The ascent ranges from hardly detectable to moderate. One 8-year-old rated the hike a 9 out of 10, deducting one point because he got a couple of bug bites and because there were a few slippery spots.

The trail begins on a state conservation easement called the Conifer Easement Lands. Following the red NYSDEC markers, the path heads up a steady incline through a mixed hardwood forest that fills with dappled sunlight on a nice day. Several stone water bars angle across the trail, stabilizing it during periods of heavy rain. Intermittent stone steps also aid the climb on this wide, obvious path. Don't be startled if you flush a couple of grouse walking through this classic upland habitat.

At 0.4 miles, the incline mellows as it crosses into the state wild forest in the Adirondack Preserve.

The route soon turns up again, though nothing extreme, as it crosses intermittent lengths of slab. Rock and log steps aid the ascent. The trail is older and more worn in this area, but the footing is still good. It zigs right around a big, round boulder, then zags back left. A birch tree with massive roots reaches over a low rock outcropping by the trail, one of a number of trees growing on top of boulders or ledges on this hike.

At 0.7 miles, the trail crosses a patch of slab and then some puncheon over a potentially muddy spot as it levels off.

At 0.9 miles, the trail climbs past a rock outcropping that forms a low wall on the left. Then the grade flattens as it goes around the wall. A short time later, you have a choice to climb up a rock chimney or circumnavigate it on a switchback.

The summit, at 1.1 miles, is just beyond a short spur to a bench perched on a viewpoint to the northwest. There is another bench that also looks west, but the fire tower is the main show. It stands atop the highest point on a large patch of rock slab, close to the former watcher's cabin. The summit clearing is the result of forest fires many years ago. The tower was in disrepair for a number of years until the Friends of Mount Arab, a local nonprofit organization, restored it. More recently, the watcher's cabin has also been restored and now serves as a two-room museum giving the history of Arab

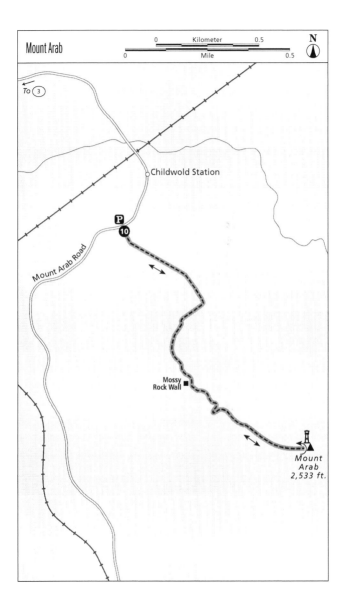

Mount Arab

To (3)

Childwold Station

Mount Arab Road

P
10

Mossy
Rock Wall

Mount
Arab
2,533 ft.

N

Kilometer
0   0.5
Mile
0   0.5

Mountain, background information on fire towers in the Adirondack Park, and a peek into the life of those who manned the tower during its heyday.

Though the summit clearing is hemmed in by red spruce and mountain ash, there is a 360-degree view from atop the tower. Mount Arab Lake and Eagle Crag Lake are below to the southwest. Tupper Lake and Raquette Pond are the large bodies of water dotted with islands to the east, with the High Peaks beyond in the distance. Mount Matumbla stands due north.

The true summit marked by a USGS benchmark— a circular brass disc—is on an open flat bit of bedrock to the north of the tower.

Return to the trailhead by the same route.

Miles and Directions

0.0 From the trailhead, follow red NYSDEC markers, climbing moderately.

0.4 Enter the Adirondack Forest Preserve, traversing through upland forest.

0.7 Cross puncheon over a potentially muddy spot.

0.9 Climb past and then around the end of a low rock wall.

1.1 Summit. Climb the fire tower, check out the fire watcher's cabin, then return by same route.

2.2 Arrive back at the trailhead.

11 Goodman Mountain

A family-friendly and dog-friendly hike to an open rock summit with a fine backcountry view.

Total distance: 3.4 miles
Type of hike: Out and back
Highest point: 2,178 feet
Vertical gain: 593 feet
Hiking time: About 2.5 hours

Canine compatibility: Dog-friendly. Dogs should be on leash.
Map: USGS Little Tupper Lake Quad

Finding the trailhead: From the junction of NY 3 and NY 30 in Tupper Lake, go 9.5 miles south on NY 30. The trailhead and hiker parking lot are on the left. **Trailhead GPS:** N44 11.571' / W74 53.587'

The Hike

Goodman Mountain, in the Horseshoe Lake Wild Forest, is the longest hike of the Tupper Lake Triad, which also includes Mount Arab and Coney Mountain. Hike all three, and you'll earn a patch and bragging rights. If you're new to hiking or hiking with young children, Goodman is an ideal outing that takes you to a lovely bald spot with an expansive view. It's also a mountain that makes one ponder an issue much bigger than this small but delightful backcountry destination. Originally called Litchfield Mountain, it was renamed Goodman Mountain in 2002 in honor of Andrew Goodman, who spent his childhood summers in Tupper Lake and enjoyed climbing the mountain with his family. In 1964, Goodman, a white 20-year-old college student, went to Mississippi to encourage black people to register to vote. Shortly after arriving in Mississippi, he was murdered by the Ku

Klux Klan. The trail up Goodman Mountain was completed in 2014, the 50th anniversary of Andrew Goodman's death.

Unlike most trails in the Adirondack Park, the first half of this hike is paved because it used to be a road from Tupper Lake to Long Lake. As a result, the grade is gentle at first, and wheelchair accessible for the first quarter mile. Motor vehicles are no longer allowed.

From the sign-in box, the route crosses a substantial footbridge over Cold Brook, following red NYSDEC trail markers, into a mixed hardwood forest. Maple trees are among the dominant species. During fall foliage season, the colors on this route are stunning to behold.

At 0.3 miles, the path turns uphill more noticeably, though nothing extreme. During the spring, purple trillium and clintonia are among the wildflowers blooming along this stretch of trail.

The pavement becomes rougher as you climb. At 0.7 miles, the route levels off again and turns left at a sign that says, "Trail," with an arrow that points the way. You leave the pavement, heading up stone steps toward a large half-buried boulder that resembles the bow of a sinking ship. As you continue to climb, several more glacial erratics (boulders) dot the peaceful, airy woods.

At 1 mile, the trail bends decisively to the left again as it reaches a plateau. The footing becomes a mosaic of tree roots and rock, but remains generally good under the towering trees.

At 1.4 miles, you ascend more stone steps as you continue uphill. A few minutes later, the trail dips slightly through a garden of boulders before the last push to the top.

At 1.7 miles, the summit appears in front of you, along with an impressive view. Acre after acre of forest carpets the valleys and hills with little sign of civilization. The sizable pond to the west is Horseshoe Lake. Of the shorter hikes in

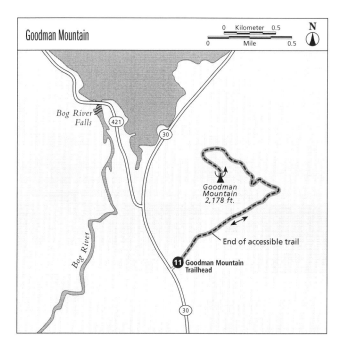

the Adirondack Park, this one is a local favorite because of its reasonable grade, the large deciduous trees along the way, and the idyllic open top.

Return to the trailhead by the same route.

Miles and Directions

- **0.0** Start by crossing a bridge and continue into the woods on a paved path (former road).
- **0.7** Turn left, leaving the pavement and heading up stone steps.
- **1.0** Bend left, reaching a plateau.
- **1.4** Ascend more rock steps then dip through a boulder garden.
- **1.7** Summit. Return by the same route.
- **3.4** Arrive back at the trailhead.

12 Lyon Mountain

A woodland walk then a fun scramble up rocks to a fire tower with views into Canada, Vermont, and the Adirondack High Peaks.

Total distance: 6.4 miles
Type of hike: Out and back
Highest point: 3,830 feet
Vertical gain: 1,904 feet
Hiking time: About 5 hours

Canine compatibility: Dog-friendly. Do not allow your dog on the fire tower.
Map: USGS Lyon Mountain Quad

Finding the trailhead: From the junction of NY 374 and Standish Road in the hamlet of Lyon Mountain, take NY 374 east for 3.6 miles. Turn right (south) on Chazy Lake Road. Go 1.7 miles. Turn right on a seasonal dirt road (formerly called Lowenburg Road) at the NYSDEC sign for Lyon Mountain. Go 0.9 miles to the end of the road. The trailhead is on the left, a former continuation of the dirt road. Parking is on the right. **Trailhead GPS:** N44 43.424' / W73 50.519'

The Hike

Lyon Mountain is only 171 feet short of making the 4,000-footer list. It is a monadnock—a prominent peak that stands alone—about 30 miles west of Plattsburgh, crowning the southwestern shore of Chazy Lake. From 1870 to 1967, iron ore was mined from the mountain. Considered some of the finest iron ore in the world, it was used to construct the Golden Gate Bridge in San Francisco. Nine years after the mine opened, Verplanck Colvin located the headquarters for his Adirondack survey at Lyon Mountain (the hamlet at the base of the mountain). In 2005 the state of New York purchased 20,000 acres of land in the northern Adirondacks, including Lyon Mountain, from the Nature Conservancy for $9.8 million, which was about the time that restoration work on the fire tower began.

Though the trail up Lyon Mountain is longer than 6 miles round-trip, it feels easier to hike than many shorter ascents. The route described here was cut in 2009, replacing the original, washed-out bee-line to the summit. It has lots of modern-day switchbacks and a moderate incline until it meets the original trail just below the tower. The panorama from atop Lyon Mountain is the king of views in the northern Adirondacks. You can see the highest peaks in both New York and Vermont from atop its fire tower as well as Montreal, Quebec, on a clear day.

From the parking lot, continue up the dirt road on foot, which quickly turns into uneven cobblestones. The route (red NYSDEC markers) is a wide, unmaintained jeep road that rises through a hardwood forest with both paper and yellow birch and striped maple in the mix.

At 0.3 miles, the trail splits briefly around a stand of paper birch, then comes to a pile of sticks and logs blocking the old trail. Turn left at the sign onto the newer route, crossing a stream on a footbridge. The path is soft and muddy but easygoing. After a long switchback, you ascend along an angled traverse to the southwest. The trail bends left as it rounds another switchback and levels off on a lazy arc to the right. But it soon resumes climbing through the ferns and forest, heading to the southwest.

After a slight downhill, it skirts a hillside, passing mature hemlocks. After one particularly muddy section, stepping stones aid the climb.

At 0.7 miles the trail dips again, crossing a stream on a second footbridge. It then begins climbing again, though moderately and at the same angle to the southwest.

At 1 mile, you cross the first lengths of slab where a couple of fir trees have toppled over, exposing the bedrock below. The trail bends right, still climbing moderately, then traverses more rock-strewn mud.

After another long switchback, the trail zigzags through the forest. The canopy opens briefly as you wind through a small clearing of ferns. Then it heads downhill past a large glacial erratic on the right side of the trail. This huge boulder has a cleft in its side, creating a shallow overhang.

The downhill is short. The trail levels off, then passes over a small freshet. After a couple more switchbacks, it ascends more persistently. It bends to the north through a grove of birch and ferns, entering the lower boreal. Hemlocks and paper birch take over the forest mix.

As you zigzag upward, the elevation gain becomes more evident. You begin to see sky through the trees on your left, rather than just above the treetops. The trail passes a moss-topped boulder, which forms a short wall next to the trail on a longish traverse, coming to a junction with the old route at 2.5 miles. Turn left, heading up the broad, eroded trail.

The trail is steep and heads directly up the side of the mountain. It's eroded and uneven, with exposed roots winding across the path among the rocks. Indian pipe, asters, and clintonia peek from among the rocks and roots.

At 2.7 miles, the trail passes the remains of the small fire-watcher's cabin, of which only two front steps, two footings, and the foundation wall on the uphill side remain. Beyond the cabin site the eroded, braided trail continues its persistent ascent up the steepest section yet. It's also the wettest and muddiest section after a rainstorm, but the view of Chazy Lake, which starts to appear behind you to the northeast, helps keep enthusiasm high for reaching the summit.

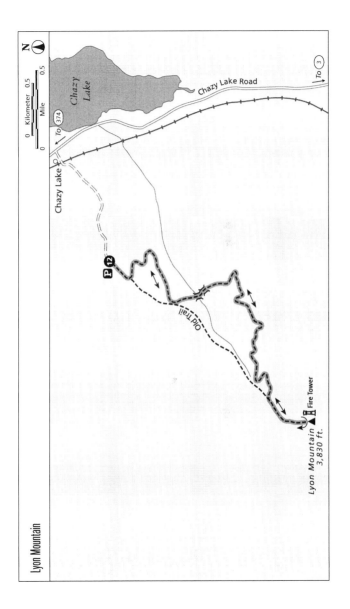

Lyon Mountain

At 2.8 miles, the steep pitch begins to mellow. There are more sections of slab underfoot. As the trail levels off, the trees become noticeably slimmer.

The fire tower looms over the treetops at 3.2 miles. The 35-foot tower sits on open bedrock on the broad summit. It was built in 1917 and served until 1988. There is a 360-degree view, but the eastern panorama, which includes Lake Champlain, plus Mount Mansfield and Camel's Hump across the water in Vermont, draws your eye the most. The High Peaks crown the horizon to the south. Chazy Lake is the large, close body of water to the northeast. The white windmills that dot the countryside to the north produce electricity for the surrounding communities. After looking around, descend the tower and head toward the lake view, where there are open ledges and several perfect picnic spots. The view is much better here than on the west side of the summit, which is covered with thin, scrubby trees.

Return to the trailhead by the same route.

Miles and Directions

0.0 Start at the trailhead. Head up the former jeep road.

0.3 Turn left onto the newer route, crossing a stream on a footbridge.

0.7 Dip down to a second footbridge over another stream.

1.0 Pass over slab where fallen trees have peeled the soil away.

2.5 Turn left at the junction with the old route, climbing the wide, washed-out trail.

2.7 Pass the remains of the fire-watcher's cabin.

2.8 The pitch mellows.

3.2 Fire tower. Return by the same route.

6.4 Arrive back at the trailhead.

13 Saint Regis Mountain

A relatively easy hike, considering the mileage, to a restored fire tower and a fantastic view of the Saint Regis Canoe Area.

Total distance: 6.6 miles
Type of hike: Out and back
Highest point: 2,858 feet
Vertical gain: 1,260 feet
Hiking time: About 5.5 hours

Canine compatibility: Dog-friendly. Do not allow your dog on the fire tower.
Map: USGS Saint Regis Mountain Quad

Finding the trailhead: At the junction of NY 86 and NY 30 in Paul Smiths, head north on NY 30. Go 100 yards, then turn left (west) on Keese Mills Road. Go 2.5 miles. The trailhead parking lot is on the left side of the road just past the turn for Topridge Road. Walk 0.1 miles down Topridge Road to the trailhead. **Trailhead GPS:** N44 25.923' / W74 18.011'

The Hike

Saint Regis Mountain is a short hike if you take a boat across Upper Saint Regis Lake, but if you must go by car, you'll need to follow the full route, which is described here. It's over 6 miles, but it's easy terrain-wise, as most of the route is the approach to the mountain, not the ascent. And it's very pretty, especially when the leaves reach their peak color in the fall (late September here) due to the many maples in the forest mix. There's a fantastic view from the summit plateau, whether you climb the fire tower or not. Although on the long side for young children, this is a great hike for older kids and dogs.

From the parking lot on Keese Mills Road, cross over the metal bridge on foot and walk the 0.1 miles down the dirt road to the trailhead, which is on the right. From the sign-in box, cross a streamlet on a long footbridge and climb a few stone steps following the red NYSDEC markers. The trail bends left (south) and continues to climb moderately up the small hillside. It quickly flattens out and then dips past a small grassy wetland on your left. The footing is smooth as you wind through the classic mixed northern forest.

At 0.2 miles (from the trailhead), the trail swings right (northwest) on another easy, short climb and then levels off on a woods road. A moment later watch for a short detour over a large low boulder. The woods road goes straight, but it's blocked by sticks. The trail merges with the road again on the other side of the elongated boulder and then narrows to a footpath over a length of slab as it continues deeper into the forest, climbing moderately.

At 0.8 miles, the path passes through a grove of mature hemlocks where the ground is clear of flora and debris except for a soft carpet of duff. Then the trail begins a long, gradual downhill, and hardwoods return to the mix. Eventually the path bends to the south on a sustained undulating traverse.

At 2 miles, the trail crosses a footbridge over a pretty streamlet and bends to the southwest. Soon afterward it finally begins to climb the mountain. Though a steady pitch, the footing is smooth and not overly strenuous. After a dip, the climb resumes, now with roots and stones strewn along the path.

At 2.4 miles, the trail climbs more persistently up through a young forest onto the shoulder of the mountain. A few stone steps aid the ascent.

At 2.6 miles, the trail bends northwest up a much longer stone staircase and then more stone steps just beyond a low, mossy rock outcropping. Look back to glimpse Spitfire Lake through the trees. You notice the elevation gain as the forest brightens and the canopy thins.

The ascent is direct, passing under another low rock wall, and then heads up through a well-traveled, eroded section. After scrambling over a rock jumble, the ascent eases on a small high shelf before winding around the north side of the mountain.

At 3.1 miles, a spur trail on the right leads to a view to the west and north. The fire tower is just above you at 3.3 miles.

The 35-foot-tall tower was erected in 1910, then closed in 1990, one of the last manned towers in the Adirondacks. For many years, the state of New York intended to remove the tower because it was considered a nonconforming structure in a wilderness area, but it was also listed on the registry for National Historic Places. The Friends of Saint Regis Mountain Fire Tower collected over 2,500 signatures, successfully petitioning the state to allow the tower to be restored for the enjoyment of hikers. In 2016, renovations to the tower were completed, and it is once again open. Whether you climb to the tower's observation cabin or relax on the broad expanse of rock below it, you'll love the unobstructed view of the 19,000-acre Saint Regis Canoe Area, the largest wilderness canoe area in the northeastern United States and the only one in New York.

Return to the trailhead by the same route.

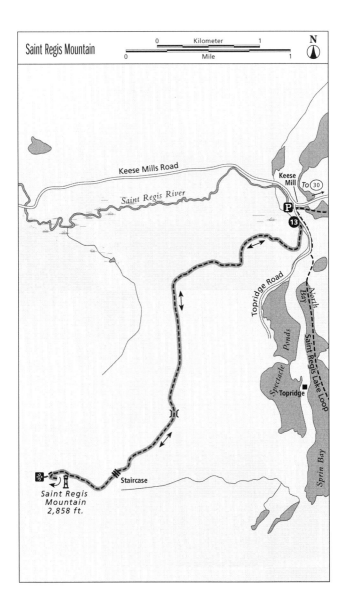

Saint Regis Mountain

Keese Mills Road

Saint Regis River

Keese Mill

To 30

P

13

Topridge Road

North Bay

Saint Regis Lake Loop

Spectacle Ponds

Topridge

Sprin Bay

Staircase

Saint Regis
Mountain
2,858 ft.

0 Kilometer 1

0 Mile 1

N

Miles and Directions

0.0   Start at the trailhead. Enter the woods on a footbridge.

0.2   Swing right and climb a short way to a woods road.

0.8   Pass through a grove of tall hemlocks.

2.0   Cross a footbridge and begin climbing.

2.4   Reach a shoulder of the mountain.

2.6   Continue the steep ascent aided by stone steps.

3.1   Turn right onto a short spur to a rock outcropping just below the summit for a view to the north and west.

3.3   Summit. Return by the same route.

6.6   Arrive back at the trailhead. Walk the short way down Topridge Road back to your car.

The Central Adirondacks lie at the geographic heart of the Adirondack Park. Two United States presidents have come to this region. In 1892 Grover Cleveland, no longer in office, visited a famous local guide named Alvah Dunning on the edge of Blue Mountain Lake. In 1901, Theodore Roosevelt was near North Creek when he received word that President McKinley had died and that he was now president of the United States. Among the other famous people to visit the area, Thomas Edison used to spend his summers in Blue Mountain Lake, where he wired a local hotel called Prospect House, making it the first hotel in the world to have electricity.

While the mountains of the Central Adirondacks are under the lorded 4,000-foot mark, there are a number of bald summits or fire towers with 360-degree views. Though the region was heavily logged, the forests have grown back and are now rich with wildflowers and wildlife. Indian Lake lies near the center of the region, but there are dozens of other lakes and ponds, thirty-six in the Siamese Ponds Wilderness alone. Several well-known rivers, including the Hudson and the East Branch Sacandaga Rivers, also flow through the area.

14 Blue Mountain

One of the most popular hikes in the Adirondacks, up a well-worn trail to a fire tower and a 360-degree view.

Total distance: 4.4 miles
Type of hike: Out and back
Highest point: 3,750 feet
Vertical gain: 1,535 feet
Hiking time: About 4 hours

Canine compatibility: Dog-friendly. Dogs should be on leash. Do not allow your dog on the fire tower.
Map: USGS Blue Mountain Quad

Finding the trailhead: From the junction of NY 28, NY 28N, and NY 30 in the hamlet of Blue Mountain Lake, go 1.4 miles north on NY 28N/NY 30. The trailhead and parking area are on the right (east) side of the road at the top of the hill just beyond the Adirondack Experience (museum).

From the junction where NY 28N splits from NY 30/28N, go west on 28N for 9.2 miles. **Note:** The trailhead is shared with the route to Tirrel Pond. The path up Blue Mountain is on the right (west) side of the parking lot. **Trailhead GPS:** N43 52.475' / W74 25.851'

The Hike

Blue Mountain is one of the most climbed mountains in the Adirondack Park. About 15,000 people ascend to its fire tower each year. The climb is persistent up an eroded trail that's mainly rock cobbles or slab. Save this one for a dry day as the rock can be slippery when it's wet.

The route up Blue Mountain begins as a woods road, heading east and climbing gently. At 0.4 miles, the trail crosses a wet area on puncheon steps, then narrows to a footpath, though the path is still obvious and well used.

As you climb through the mixed northern forest, the maples become fewer and the birch and hemlock increase. Painted trillium, hobblebushes, and clintonia bloom beside the trail in early June.

At 0.9 miles, you cross a pretty stream flowing over some slab. Beyond the stream the path gets steeper. Rock steps aid the ascent, and the canopy gets thinner.

At 1.2 miles, the route swings east toward a rise of land, then ascends some rubble and slab. The climb is now more sustained—the "real" climb up the mountain—as spruce and other conifers take over the forest mix. The trail is worn to bedrock for most of the steady, steep ascent, which can be slippery if wet.

At 1.9 miles, as you near the summit area, the path winds through the stunted evergreens of the boreal forest. You start to see sky and hints of a view through the trees on your left.

At 2 miles, the ascent mellows as you traverse a mud hole and then across a short bog bridge. Abundant patches of sphagnum moss carpet the forest floor.

At 2.2 miles, a sign, "Toilet," nailed to a tree, points to a privy on your left about 20 yards off the trail. The 35-foot tower, a state and national historic landmark, is just around the bend in the middle of a huge open, flat area. In 1873, during Verplanck Colvin's survey of the Adirondack Mountains, Colvin's crew put up a signal tower atop Blue Mountain that was greatly valued for its south-central location. A wooden fire tower replaced the signal tower in 1907, which in turn was replaced by the current steel tower in 1917.

The large concrete slab directly below the tower was the foundation of the first fire watcher's cabin. Another, later watcher's cabin, plus a radio tower, a cell phone tower, and a

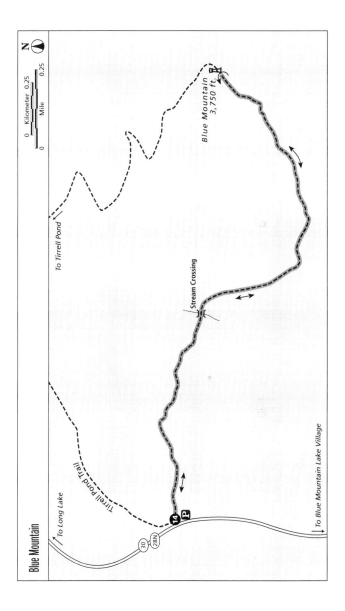

Blue Mountain

To Long Lake

Tirrell Pond Trail

To Tirrell Pond

Blue Mountain
3,750 ft.

Stream Crossing

30
(28N)

To Blue Mountain Lake Village

0   Kilometer 0.25

0   0.25
Mile

N

radar station dating back to the Cold War era are in the trees near the fire tower, though all are closed to the public.

The fire tower, which operated until 1990, is open to hikers and worth the climb to its cabin. The view from the tower is an Adirondack favorite, with Blue Mountain Lake and Raquette Lake to the west and the High Peaks on the horizon to the northeast. Snowy Mountain and Wakely Mountain, both with fire towers, lie to the south. But more impressive than the peaks is the amount of water all around you. There seems to be more lakes than land as you gaze across this region of the Adirondacks.

Return to the trailhead by the same route.

Miles and Directions

0.0 From the trailhead, follow the red NYSDEC markers toward Blue Mountain.

0.4 Cross a wet area on puncheon.

0.9 Cross a stream flowing over slab.

1.2 Swing east and begin the real climb.

1.9 Wind through stunted, thinning evergreens.

2.2 Fire tower. Return by the same route.

4.4 Arrive back at the trailhead and parking area.

15 Castle Rock Loop

A short hike with big rewards including a rock labyrinth, cave, and clifftop view of Blue Mountain Lake.

Total distance: 3.7 miles
Type of hike: Loop
Highest point: 2,438 feet
Vertical gain: 711 feet
Hiking time: About 2.5 hours

Canine compatibility: Dog-friendly. Dogs should be on leash.
Map: USGS Deerland Quad (summit), Blue Mountain Lake Quad (trailhead)

Finding the trailhead: From Long Lake, take NY 30/NY 28N southwest for 10 miles. Turn right on Maple Lodge Road. Go 1.1 miles to the trailhead. The road narrows and turns to dirt then becomes pavement again as you go through part of Syracuse University's Minnowbrook Conference Center campus. Watch for the hiker parking on the left across from the hiker registration box. **Trailhead GPS:** N43 52.383' / W74 27.023'

The Hike

Located in the Blue Mountain Wild Forest, Castle Rock Mountain is one of those hiking gems that you'll do over and over because the hike is interesting, good exercise but not too difficult, and the view at the summit of Blue Mountain Lake is stunning. The hike starts at the sign-in box in the heart of the Minnowbrook Conference Center, a former Adirondack great camp that was gifted to Syracuse University and now serves as a retreat, meeting facility, and education center for the college and other groups.

From the sign-in box, head down a gravel road passing several driveways. At 0.2 miles, bear right at an apparent fork.

Left is actually another driveway. Don't worry about the "Private" sign. This is a public right-of-way for hikers with red NYSDEC trail markers on the telephone poles beside the road. The road heads easily uphill. Another 0.1 miles later, bear right again (left is private), now on a broad woods road. The way becomes a little more cobbled and soon parallels a brook on your left.

At 0.4 miles, you come to the junction at a footbridge over the brook. You will close the loop here later. Turn left over the bridge now following yellow NYSDEC discs. The route continues gently uphill on a woods road. It bends right, narrows to a truer footpath, then heads gradually downhill. At a large boulder it bends right again and levels off as you head around the wetlands by Chubb Pond, which you can see through the trees.

At 0.8 miles, the trail to Blue Mountain Lake departs to your left. Bear right crossing over a seasonal stream, still following the yellow trail markers which will take you to the top. The climb is more noticeable, and the trail gets rockier as you pass a huge glacial erratic (boulder) deposited over 10,000 years ago after the last ice age receded.

At 1.3 miles, you crest a hump of bedrock then head downhill. Several more mammoth boulders lie in the woods to your right. Soon you reach a tall rock wall. The trail bends sharply left below the wall, which is actually another giant boulder. Behind it lies a small open area framed by the backside of the boulder on one side and an overhung cliff on the other. It's like a natural echo chamber! There's also a tall cave formed by several titanic boulders in one corner of this prehistoric sanctuary.

At the entrance to the cave sanctuary, the trail actually bends left. It does not go through the clearing or uphill at this point. The route heads through a labyrinth of giant rocks, then it begins a steady climb away from the cave. Follow the yellow markers carefully through here until the path becomes obvious again.

At 1.6 miles, you reach a T which is the top of the loop. Bear right, continuing uphill toward the rock cliff.

Before the cliff, the trail bends left and gets steeper and more washed out. It zigzags up rocks and slab, eventually coming to another boulder pile. This time, the route heads up a deep cleft in the rocks. Turn right at the top of the cleft to reach the top of the "castle" at 1.7 miles. The summit caps an 80-foot, tiered cliff perched over Blue Mountain Lake. Though the neighboring mountains certainly add to the view, the lake is the main show. From the summit's sizable open ledge, you can watch paddlers and motorboaters heading into the lake's numerous bays and inlets, enjoy a picnic, and relax.

When you're ready to go, retrace back to the junction below the cleft in the boulders, at 1.8 miles. This time, continue straight (right) to start the loop-portion of this hike. *Note:* The trail markers can be confusing at this point as both ways are marked with yellow NYSDEC discs. The main reason to make a loop is the footing. The trail is dirt and joint-friendly most of the way down. Instead of giant rocks, you see a number of impressive, mature hardwoods in the forest mix.

At 2.3 miles, you cross a stream and arrive at a junction with the Sargent Pond Trail. Turn right, following the red NYSDEC discs and the arrow for the "Castle Rock Loop." The trail becomes flatter though still descending gently. It soon follows a streamlet to a modest grassy clearing on your right, then bends left up a small rise before heading downhill again to a more substantial but seasonal stream.

The path terraces the hillside as the streambed gets further away below you. Several stretches of puncheon (low bog bridges), including one long one that makes an S through

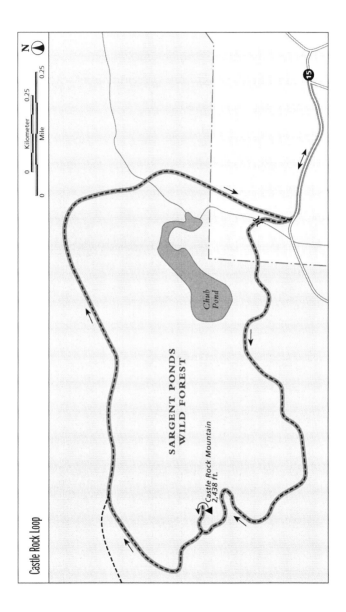

Castle Rock Loop

the woods, keep your feet drier through a number of muddy spots. You'll also cross several more small streams though they are barely a trickle by mid-summer.

At 3.3 miles, the large, grassy wetlands surrounding Chubb Pond lie on your right through the trees. The trail follows the outlet of the pond which turns into a brook by the time it reaches the footbridge you crossed earlier.

Close the loop at the trail junction by the footbridge at 3.4 miles. This time, instead of crossing the bridge, head straight, retracing the remainder of the hike back to the trailhead at 3.7 miles.

Miles and Directions

0.0 From the hiker registration box, head down a gravel road.

0.2 Bear right, avoiding a driveway and following the red trail markers on the telephone poles.

0.4 Turn left crossing a substantial footbridge.

0.8 Bear right at the junction with the Blue Mountain Lake Trail.

1.3 Cave. Bear left at the entrance to the cave "sanctuary," then head through a labyrinth of boulders.

1.6 Turn right at the T, which marks the top of the loop.

1.7 Summit. Retrace back to the top of the loop.

1.8 Continue straight at the junction on the Castle Rock Loop Trail.

2.3 Turn right at the junction with the Sargent Pond Trail.

3.3 Pass by the expansive wetlands around Chubb Pond.

3.4 Close the loop at the footbridge. Head straight, retracing your steps down the dirt road.

3.7 Arrive back at the trailhead and parking area.

16 Goodnow Mountain

This modest hike climbs to a 60-foot fire tower with breathtaking views of the surrounding mountains, lakes, and ponds.

Total distance: 4.4 miles
Type of hike: Out and back
Highest point: 2,664 feet
Vertical gain: 1,106 feet
Hiking time: About 3.5 hours

Canine compatibility: Dog-friendly. Dogs should be on leash. Do not allow your dog on the fire tower.
Map: USGS Newcomb Quad

Finding the trailhead: At the junction of NY 30 and NY 28N in Long Lake, travel east on NY 28N toward Newcomb for 11 miles. Turn right at the white sign for Goodnow Mountain (not a NYSDEC sign) to find the trailhead and parking area.

From Newcomb, the trailhead is 3.3 miles west of Newcomb Central School, on the left. *Note:* Goodnow Mountain is a day-use area, open daily from sunrise to sunset. **Trailhead GPS:** N43 58.178' / W74 12.864'

The Hike

Named for Sylvester Goodnow, a homesteader who settled at the base of the mountain in the 1820s, Goodnow Mountain is the only hike in this book that is not maintained by the NYSDEC, though the state built the fire tower on its summit. The mountain is located in the Huntington Wildlife Forest, which is owned by the State University of New York (SUNY) College of Environmental Science and Forestry in Syracuse. The forest is a field station for wildlife research and ecology studies. The trail is maintained jointly by SUNY and the Town of Newcomb. Camping, hunting, and plant collecting are not allowed.

Follow the red markers, some with black arrows, into the woods. As you climb, you also pass by yellow numbered markers, some upright, some tilted, and others knocked over, remnants of a former nature trail up the mountain.

The wide trail climbs moderately from the sign-in box. You come almost immediately to a highly constructed wooden staircase with a handrail. Above the stairs, it bends right (north) and flattens, crossing a wet area. At 0.1 miles, it passes over a streamlet on a bog bridge, heads downhill, and crosses another length of puncheon before resuming the climb.

The smooth trail rolls past towering beech, birch, maple, and hemlock. At 0.75 miles, the trail turns upward and soon crosses another bog bridge. Partway up the slope a mature yellow birch grows atop a large rock. Its roots sprawl down the sides of the rock like a giant octopus reaching its tentacles toward the ground. Above the "octopus rock," the climb becomes more persistent but mellows ten minutes later as it bends to the right (south).

At 0.9 miles, bear right up one switchback, rather than straight up. Straight up is an old washed-out section of trail that is now blocked off with fallen logs.

At 1.8 miles, the trail ascends up a long length of slab. It traverses a long arcing bog bridge and then comes to the concrete foundation of a former cabin. You'll also pass a pile of wood boards and old pieces of roof, the ruins of another old cabin.

After crossing more puncheon, the route ascends in waves toward the summit. Evergreens take over the forest mix as you sense the elevation gain. The trail narrows as you reach

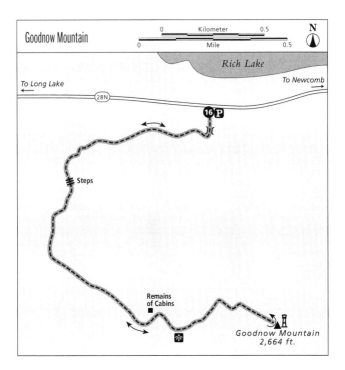

a high shoulder of the mountain. At 2 miles, you come to a tilted, perch-like slab of open rock on your right, but the view is blocked by young maples, birches, and a few taller fir trees. The trail dips, then makes its final, moderate climb to the summit.

At 2.2 miles, the fire tower crowns the open rock. From its steel cabin, you're rewarded with a 360-degree panorama that includes Rich Lake below you to the north and the Seward and Santanoni Ranges, Algonquin Peak, and Mounts Colden and Marcy in the distance.

The fire watcher's cabin is just beyond the tower. Look in the window to see its interior as it was when it was still in use. A sample of the fire watcher's log is on the door, along with a couple of historic photos. George Shaughnessy, the watcher here from 1930 to 1934, spent his honeymoon in the cabin in 1931.

Return by the same route.

Miles and Directions

0.0 Climb up log ties and a wood staircase just above the sign-in box.

0.1 Cross a streamlet on a bog bridge.

0.75 Octopus rock. Continue climbing moderately.

0.9 Bear right up a single switchback where the trail was rerouted.

1.8 Pass a concrete foundation and remains of two cabins.

2.0 Pass a slab perch with no view.

2.2 Fire tower. Return by the same route.

4.4 Arrive back at the trailhead and parking area.

17 Moxham Mountain

A relatively new trail through a peaceful hardwood forest, then over a number of open ledges to an expansive view of mountains, backcountry ponds, and the Hudson River.

Total distance: 5.2 miles
Type of hike: Out and back
Highest point: 2,441 feet
Vertical gain: 1,150 feet
Hiking time: About 3.5 hours

Canine compatibility: Dog-friendly. Dogs should be on leash.
Map: USGS Minerva Quad (summit), Dutton Mountain Quad (trailhead)

Finding the trailhead: Take exit 26 off I-87 onto US 9 south. Turn right on Olmstedville Road toward Minerva. At the junction with AP Morse Memorial Highway (CR 30), turn right on AP Morse Highway. Go 2.4 miles. Turn left on Town Shed Road (CR 37). Go 0.2 miles to the junction with the Roosevelt Marcy Memorial Highway. Continue straight following the sign to "Moxam Mountain Trailhead" (different spelling of "Moxham"). The road is now 14th Road. After 2.1 miles, 14th Road turns to dirt. At 2.3 miles, the small hiker parking lot and trailhead are on your left by a small sign that says "Trailhead Parking." A second parking area is slightly farther on your right. **Trailhead GPS:** N43 46.227' / W74 00.720'

The Hike

Located in the Vanderwhacker Mountain Wild Forest, Moxham Mountain is a minor peak with major rewards for hikers, namely expansive views from a dozen different ledgy overlooks. The route, known as the Moxham Mountain Trail, is named for Robert Moxham, a surveyor in the area during the late 1700s who purportedly fell off one of these cliffs.

Don't worry. While the drop-offs are precipitous, there's plenty of space on each rock shelf to keep away from the edge and still enjoy the panoramas.

The Moxham Mountain Trail, which opened in 2012, is relatively new by Adirondacks standards. It was constructed by the NYSDEC in conjunction with the Student Conservation Association (SCA). The SCA is a conservation corps that started in the 1950s. Its members "protect and restore national parks, marine sanctuaries, cultural landmarks and community green spaces in all 50 states" while gaining a sense of environmental stewardship from these hands-on experiences.

The route begins on the northwest side of the mountain. From the sign-in box which is a few steps into the woods from the trailhead, the path heads south, climbing moderately through peaceful hardwoods. Though some roots crisscross the path, the footing is generally good as the trail winds through the forest, bending casually left and right. The only sounds are the wind, birds, and the occasional chattering chipmunk.

At 0.5 miles, the trail swings left up a steeper pitch, where you'll cross the first of many lengths of shallow rock slab. The grade soon eases again as you come to the first of the viewpoints, mainly of a nearby hill. The trail now parallels the ledges buffered by blueberry and other low bushes.

After re-entering the woods, the trail begins a long descent. At 1 mile, you cross an unreliable stream, which is the outlet from an old beaver pond. The route heads uphill again on a moderate grade then flattens, terracing through the woods on a southerly course.

At 1.3 miles, the trail hugs a large boulder, one of many glacial erratics strewn throughout this part of the forest. Then the route drops down to another stream before turning uphill more steeply for a moment.

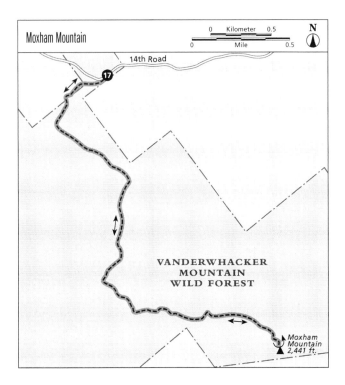

At 1.6 miles, the path turns left heading toward a low rock wall which has cracked apart vertically in several spots. At the base of the wall, the path turns right, passing a large rock "seat" en route to a bald spot and the first of many views of Gore Mountain's ski trails to the south. The trail bends slightly left away from the view, passing a balancing boulder that one hiker likened to "an oversized exercise ball" before heading back into the woods.

The route crosses more rock slab including a rib of bedrock as it dips and rises a few times, passing by more viewpoints. At 2.3 miles, at yet another of these ledge-top breaks, you see the sheer cliffs of Moxham's summit to your left (east). The hulking rock face looks intimidating, but the rest of the hike remains reasonable, loosely following the cliff line but in the woods.

At 2.6 miles, you reach the summit. The metal rings near the benchmark are remnants of Verplanck Colvin's Adirondack survey. Colvin visited this summit four times between 1872 and 1896. It's not a 360-degree view, but it's an eye-popping one. Clear, Long, and Fuller Ponds lie below you, with much of the Central Adirondacks to the west. Gore Mountain dominates the view to the southwest, and the Hudson River, which looks like a silver ribbon, is visible to the southeast. The large scar west of Gore is the Barton Mine on the side of Ruby Mountain.

Return by the same route.

Miles and Directions

0.0 Begin at the trailhead on 14th Road.

0.5 Climb up a short, steep pitch with slab underfoot.

1.0 Cross a seasonal stream.

1.3 Pass a large boulder (glacial erratic) next to the trail.

1.6 Pass under a rock wall with vertical cracks and a large "seat" in the rock.

2.3 See the summit cliffs from a ledge-top bald spot.

2.6 Summit. Return by the same route.

5.2 Arrive back at the trailhead.

The Southern Adirondacks encompass the section of the Adirondack Park south of NY 8 between Prospect and Speculator, plus the land in the southern half of the Wilcox Lake Wild Forest between Speculator and Lake George village. This is the region closest to large population centers, particularly Albany, the state capital, yet the trails are not crowded, especially midweek.

The Southern region is best characterized by braided rivers and creeks that wind their way between the lakes and ponds that dot the hilly countryside. The Silver Lake Wilderness is the only designated wilderness area in the region. Most of the backcountry is contained in Ferris Lake Wild Forest, Shaker Mountain Wild Forest, and Wilcox Wild Forest.

Because the topography of the Southern Adirondacks is gentler than in the heart of the Adirondack Park, the hikes here are particularly nice for families who are either new to hiking or who don't want to make a full day of it. The routes described here are among the classics of the region. Each offers a beautiful view, a pleasant woodland walk, and just enough topography to keep things interesting.

18 Crane Mountain–Crane Pond Loop

A fun climb up rocks, slab, and a couple of ladders to an eye-popping view of the region, then a gentle descent to a small remote pond.

Total distance: 3.1 miles
Type of hike: Lollipop
Highest point: 2,851 feet
Vertical gain: 1,387 feet
Hiking time: About 3 hours

Canine compatibility: Not dog-friendly due to ladders near summit
Map: USGS Johnsburg Quad

Finding the trailhead: At the junction of US 9 and NY 418 in Warrensburg, go 3.6 miles west on NY 418 toward Thurman. At a cluster of signs on the right, turn right (northwest) on Athol Road, following the signs toward the town hall and Veteran's Field. Go 1.1 miles to a T. Turn right (northeast) onto Cameron Road. Go 0.9 miles, then bear right (north) on Glen/Athol Road. Go 1.4 miles, then turn left on Valley Road. Go 4.6 miles, then turn left on Garnet Lake Road South. Go 1.3 miles, then turn right on Ski Hi Road (dirt). Go 1.9 miles. The road narrows at the top of a hill as it crosses onto forest preserve land. The road winds through a wetland and ends at the trailhead parking area.
Trailhead GPS: N43 32.239' / W73 58.034'

The Hike

The hardest part of this hike is finding the trailhead, but once there you'll enjoy this interesting climb to the summit of Crane Mountain and the pleasant walk to the pond of the same name. You begin and end on the same trail, but make a loop over the mountaintop, then down to the pond on a high shelf of the mountain, before rejoining the trail you started on.

There are two stories behind the name of the mountain and the pond, one crediting a pair of cranes that were rumored to have nested on the pond in the previous century, the other crediting a state surveyor with the last name of Crane who marked a 55-mile line that ran over the mountaintop.

Two trails depart from the sign-in box, one to Putnam Farm Junction/Crane Pond and the other to Crane Mountain/Crane Pond. **Note:** The actual name of the pond is "Crane Mountain Pond," though the sign says only "Crane Pond." Bear right (north), following the red NYSDEC markers toward Crane Mountain. The well-worn trail tilts upward over rocks and roots through a dense hardwood forest of maple, birch, and beech. The footing soon becomes a jumble of rocks as you quickly gain elevation.

You can see the neighboring hills through the trees where the trail bends left (northwest) at the base of a sizable rock face. The jumble of rocks becomes more vertical as you climb up the broad rocky slope, similar to ascending an old slide, but more stable.

At 0.5 miles, at the top of the talus, a yellow arrow points to the right up a section of smooth, low-angle slab. At the top of the slab, there is a short spur trail to a lookout to the northwest over blueberry bushes. Crane Mountain is a wild-blueberry bonanza in July.

Above the slab, the forest transitions to birch and soft-woods, and the trail changes to roots underfoot. It parallels a ledge, passing a few other spots where you can poke through to get a view. Then the trail breaks out onto an expanse of slab, part of the patchwork of rock that you can see from the road as you approach the mountain.

Head straight up the slab to the junction where the Summit Trail and the Pond Trail split. Bear right (northeast) on the Summit Trail. The path dips, then heads up another short, steep, eroded jumble of rocks and roots before reaching better footing.

At 0.8 miles, a short ladder aids the ascent up a short rock wall, then the trail flattens through a grove of hemlocks as it bends to the east.

At 1.2 miles, the trail swings back to the north up another washout, then climbs more rubble to a second, longer 24-rung ladder. Above the ladder there is an excellent view from a rocky perch to the southwest. Wildlands sprawl before you as far as you can see! From here, the trail winds up a few more steps, arriving at the summit at 1.4 miles.

The footings of an old fire tower are embedded in the rock on the summit, but there is no need for a tower to take in the incredible view. The mountains along Lake George and the Green Mountains of Vermont beyond lie to the east. Moose Mountain and Baldhead dominate the view to the south, and Blue Mountain stands guard on the far shore of Garnet Lake to the southwest.

From the summit, head north on the elongated summit ledge, which narrows to a footpath. The path begins with a gentle downhill traverse, then descends more deliberately. The trail is well used but less rocky than on the way up. It levels off as you reenter the hardwoods, becoming narrower and smoother. At 1.9 miles, it passes through a short, muddy stretch just before arriving at the eastern side of Crane Mountain Pond. Look for a short spur on your right for a peek across the 14-acre pond.

The trail bends to the west, following a yellow arrow and heading along the southern shore of the pond. You can see a nice beach and campsite across the water. If you have the time, the beach is a pleasant spot for a swim. You may see anglers casting for brook trout.

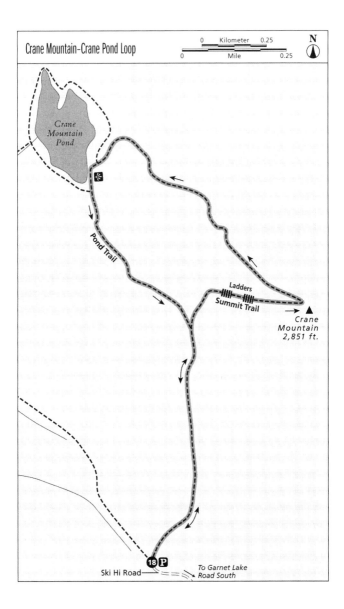

Crane Mountain-Crane Pond Loop

Kilometer

0   0.25

Mile

0   0.25

N

Crane
Mountain
Pond

Pond Trail

Ladders
Summit Trail

Crane
Mountain
2,851 ft.

18 P

Ski Hi Road

To Garnet Lake
Road South

At 2.1 miles, the trail splits. The right fork takes you to the beach and campsite. Bear left (southeast), away from the pond, heading back into the woods on the Pond Trail (no sign). It's easy to walk by this junction as the pond continually draws your attention. If you miss it, the next left also brings you back to the trailhead via the Putnam Farm Junction Trail, but it adds an extra mile to your hike.

The trail climbs moderately on a dry streambed, then smooths out. It crosses a length of puncheon through a hemlock grove, traversing a shoulder of the mountain, then, at 2.6 miles, you reach the junction with the Summit Trail, closing the loop. Bear right, retracing the last half mile down the rocky hillside, returning to the trailhead at 3.1 miles.

Miles and Directions

0.0 At the trailhead take the right trail toward Crane Mountain/ Crane Pond.

0.5 Turn right where the Pond Trail and the Summit Trail split, following the Summit Trail.

0.8 Climb a ladder up a short rock wall.

1.2 Climb another, longer ladder.

1.4 Summit. Head north along the summit ridge to descend toward the pond.

1.9 Pond. Take the short spur trail for a view across the pond, then head along the southern shore of the pond.

2.1 Bear left at the fork on the Pond Trail (no sign), heading away from the pond into the woods.

2.6 Close the loop at the junction with the Summit Trail. Turn right and retrace back to the trailhead.

3.1 Arrive back at the trailhead and parking area.

19 Hadley Mountain

A family-friendly hike to a restored fire tower and an expansive 360-degree view that includes the High Peaks, the Green Mountains (Vermont), and the Berkshires (Massachusetts) on a clear day.

Total distance: 3.6 miles
Type of hike: Out and back
Highest point: 2,651 feet
Vertical gain: 1,456 feet
Hiking time: About 3.5 hours

Canine compatibility: Dog-friendly. Do not allow your dog on the fire tower.
Maps: USGS Stony Creek Quad (summit), Conklingville Quad (trailhead)

Finding the trailhead: At the town hall in the center of Hadley, go 3 miles north on Stony Creek Road (also called Saratoga CR 1). Turn left (northwest) on Hadley Hill Road. Go 4.3 miles, then turn right (north) on Tower Road (dirt). Go 1.4 miles to the trailhead, which is on the left (west) side of the road.

From I-87, take exit 123 (Diamond Point). Turn right on Diamond Point Road, then right on US 9N. Go 0.5 miles, then turn left (west) onto NY 418, which becomes River Street then CR 3/Stony Creek Road. Go 11.1 miles from the turn off US 9N, then turn left on Grist Mill Road. Go 0.2 miles, then turn left on Hadley Hill Road. Go 0.9 miles, then turn right on Riley Hill Road which becomes Eddy Road. Go 2.5 miles, then turn right on Tower Road. Go 1.7 miles to the trailhead on the right side of the road. **Trailhead GPS:** N43 22.447' / W73 57.048'

The Hike

Located in the Wilcox Lake Wild Forest, a 140,000-acre forest preserve, Hadley Mountain is the highest point at the southern end of West Mountain, a half-mile-long ridge. It is a favorite hike in the Saratoga area for the views from its fire tower, which was placed on the National Register of Historic Places in 2001. It's a short hike, but a persistent climb.

From the trailhead, follow the red NYSDEC markers up the broad, somewhat eroded path. Lots of trailwork, including stone steps, waterbars, and log steps a little farther up the trail, help stabilize the well-trodden route. Even so, the path is cobbled between stretches of bedrock as you climb through a pretty hardwood forest. Many boulders are scattered around the forest floor. The ones next to the trail provide good places to sit and catch your breath on this steady ascent.

By 0.5 miles, the trail becomes predominantly slab—Mother Nature's sidewalk. The slab is smooth underfoot. Use caution, as it can be slick when wet. As you gain elevation, ironically fewer evergreens grow in the airy, bright forest, which becomes predominantly birch and maple.

The trail winds around several elongated switchbacks, then resumes its uphill climb in its original westerly direction. At 0.8 miles, it swings right on a long arc, then left again up more slab. It continues on similar long curves up the steep hillside before reaching more log steps and another noticeable bend to the left at 1 mile.

The trail feels steeper and steeper as it winds up the hillside, but at 1.2 miles you get some relief when the trail heads slightly downhill, then levels off. The footing turns to smoother dirt on this high shoulder of the mountain. When the ascend resumes, the pitch is more moderate up widely spaced log steps.

At 1.3 miles, you pass a small, grassy clearing with scattered trees on your right. A little farther, you pass through a gap in a rock outcropping then come to an arrow, pointing to the left. The forest soon becomes grassier and airier, and you can begin to sense a view through the trees on your left.

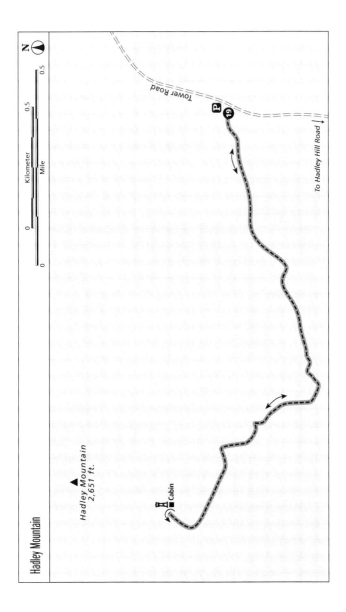

Hadley Mountain

Hadley Mountain
2,651 ft.

Cabin

Tower Road

To Hadley Hill Road

19

P

N

Kilometer

Mile

0.5

0.5

0

After another steep uphill burst, at 1.7 miles you get your first view of Great Sacandaga Lake to the southwest. Great Sacandaga Lake is a 29-mile-long reservoir formed by a dam on the Sacandaga River at its northeast end. In the late 19th and early 20th centuries, the river inundated the Albany area on several occasions, causing extensive damage. The dam has since stemmed the chance of major flood, while creating one of the largest bodies of water within the Adirondack Park.

Beyond this viewpoint, the trail climbs easily to the summit plateau, passing a spur to the former fire watcher's cabin and reaching the fire tower just beyond at 1.8 miles. The original fire tower atop Hadley Mountain was built of wood in 1916. The restored steel tower, which still stands today, replaced the original tower in 1920. From atop the tower, you can see the High Peaks to the north and the Catskills to the south. The Green Mountains in Vermont lie on the eastern horizon beyond Lake George and Lake Champlain, with the northern tip of the Berkshires to the southeast. The rolling hills of the southern Adirondacks form layers of green and blue to the west.

Return to the trailhead by the same route.

Miles and Directions

0.0 Enter the woods on a rock-strewn trail.

0.5 Ascend lengths of smooth slab.

0.8 Swing right on a long arc, then up more slab.

1.0 Bend left, then up log steps.

1.2 Dip downhill, then level off.

1.3 Pass a small grassy clearing, then follow the arrow to the left at a rock outcropping.

1.7 Pause for a view of Great Sacandaga Lake.

1.8 Fire tower. Return to the trailhead by the same route.

3.6 Arrive back at the trailhead and parking area.

20 Kane Mountain Loop

A short, kid-friendly hike to a restored fire tower and views of the Canada Lake region.

Total distance: 2.3 miles
Type of hike: Loop
Highest point: 2,180 feet
Vertical gain: 633 feet
Hiking time: About 2 hours

Canine compatibility: Dog-friendly. Do not allow your dog on the fire tower.
Map: USGS Canada Lake Quad

Finding the trailhead: From the junction of NY 10 and CR 112 north of Caroga Lake, go 2.6 miles on NY 10/29A. Turn right on Green Lake Road. Go 0.4 miles, then turn left at the sign for Kane Mountain parking (dirt) which goes into the hiker parking lot just ahead. **Trailhead GPS:** N43 10.852' / W74 30.303'

The Hike

Kane Mountain is a small peak on the northwestern side of Green Lake in the Shaker Mountain Wild Forest, a 40,500-acre preserve known for the southern terminus of the Northville–Lake Placid Trail, the "long trail" of the Adirondacks. Though Kane may be a minor peak, it is worth visiting the restored fire tower on its summit for a view of the Catskills to the south, the High Peaks to the north, and the many nearby lakes.

There are two approaches to the mountain, the Kane Mountain Trail which is actually on the eastern side of the mountain, and north of the other trail, called the East Trail. (The South Trail is closed.) The route described here is a loop that goes up the shorter East Trail and then down the slightly longer North Trail. The main reason to go up the East Trail is to get to the fire tower quicker. The North Trail is less steep and thus easier on the joints going down.

The broad East Trail departs to the left of the sign-in box, following red NYSDEC markers and immediately passing a privy. It heads northwest at first, climbing steadily on a moderate grade. While some rocks and roots litter the trail, the footing is generally good as you pass through a forest of birch, maple, poplar, and scattered hemlock, many of which reach down the sides of large rocks with their roots.

At 0.2 miles, the trail climbs a couple of short, steep sections that seem easier because of the good footing.

At 0.5 miles, you head up a stretch of slab as you continue to climb. The trail is more eroded in spots. It becomes rougher as you pass through a lawn of ferns beneath the trees, then it arcs to the right as the woods on your right become much more open.

The tower is just ahead at 0.8 miles. There's no view from its base, but the 60-foot tower lifts you above the treetops for a 360-degree view, dominated by sizable Canada Lake to the south.

Built in 1925, the Kane Mountain fire tower was used for fire detection until 1987, then abandoned. Restored in 1993 by the Canada Lake Protective Association and NYSDEC, it was the second tower, after Goodnow Mountain, to be noted for its historical importance and rejuvenated as a hiking destination in the Adirondack Park. You'll love the breeze on a hot day from this lofty lookout.

The former fire watcher's cabin is just beyond the fire tower in a grassy clearing. There's a perfect picnic rock by the cabin. If that's taken, there's another open area on the opposite side of the tower.

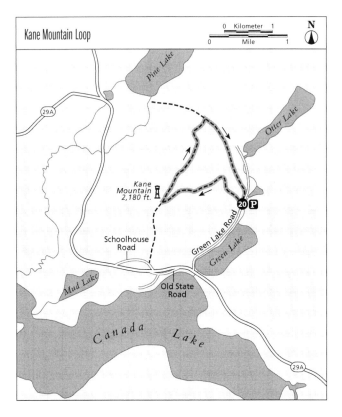

Kane Mountain Loop

Kane Mountain 2,180 ft.

Schoolhouse Road

Green Lake Road

Old State Road

Pine Lake

Otter Lake

Green Lake

Mud Lake

Canada Lake

When you're ready to depart the summit, to make a loop, follow the yellow NYSDEC markers which start to the left of the bottom step of the tower. At first, you'll pass over more slab and ferns to either side as you traverse an airy shoulder of the mountain.

At 0.9 miles, you cross a muddy spot then pass above two giant boulders before heading around the second one. Then the trail heads downhill more noticeably though the footing is good. The grade is not steep.

At 1.2 miles, the path crosses a wooded plateau and then some slab as it starts downhill again. Look for acorns sprinkled across the trail under several huge oak trees. Don't be surprised if a whitetail deer bounds away from you. The North Trail, which is less used than the East Trail, is narrower but obvious and not as worn.

After a sustained, fairly steep section, the pitch moderates again at 1.4 miles and comes to a T. Go right (uphill) at the T. There is no trail sign. The trail continues to climb on a moderate pitch until 1.7 miles. It levels off and then heads gently downhill as the forest becomes denser to either side. It eventually flattens again as you cross a mudhole on stepping stones, then dips and curves to the right.

At 2.2 miles, the route meets a woods road. Turn right at the T and then immediately pass the trail to Stewart and Indian Lakes on your left.

Close the loop just ahead, at 2.3 miles, back at the hiker parking lot.

Miles and Directions

0.0 Take the East Trail to the left of the sign-in box.

0.2 Climb a couple of short, steep sections.

0.5 Climb a stretch of slab.

0.8 Fire tower. Follow the yellow markers to descend via the North Trail.

0.9 Cross a muddy spot, then go around two giant boulders.

1.2 Cross a wooded plateau under large oak trees.

1.4 Go right at the T (no sign), heading uphill.

1.7 Continue downhill again.

2.2 Turn right at the T, then immediately pass the trail to Stewart and Indian Lakes.

2.3 Close the loop back at the hiker parking lot.

If you are looking for solitude, you'll see few other people on the trails in the West Central Adirondacks, though there are many beautiful places to visit. There are only a couple of modest mountaintops here, but a plethora of lovely lakes, rivers, ponds, swamps, and boglands await those who venture into this peaceful part of the Adirondack Park. The region was heavily logged then ravaged by fire a century ago, but the forests have largely recovered and blanket the region with an array of northern hardwoods and conifers. While the hikes in this section are not particularly long or challenging, they will take you to special places, each with a view of water and lovely in its own unique way.

When hiking the West Central Adirondacks, be sure to wear waterproof-breathable footwear as the routes may be wet, and bring a generous supply of bug repellent. The hikes described here are particularly appealing from late September through early October, when the leaves are aflame with color, though they are enjoyable any time of the year.

21 Bald Mountain (Rondaxe)

A kid-friendly hike, even for small children, with a number of cliff-top views en route to a fire tower and a view of the Fulton Chain of Lakes.

Total distance: 2 miles
Type of hike: Out and back
Highest point: 2,350 feet
Vertical gain: 412 feet
Hiking time: About 2 hours

Canine compatibility: Dog-friendly. Dogs should be on leash. Do not allow your dog on the fire tower.
Map: USGS Eagle Bay Quad

Finding the trailhead: From the Town of Webb Visitor's Center by the covered bridge in Old Forge, go 4.7 miles east on NY 28. Turn left (north) on Rondaxe Road. Go 0.1 miles. The trailhead and trailhead parking lot are on the left.

From the junction of Big Moose Road and NY 28 in Eagle Bay, go 4.6 miles west on NY 28. Turn right (north) on Rondaxe Road.
Trailhead GPS: N43 44.732' / W74 54.009'

The Hike

There are sixteen Bald Mountains in New York State. This one is tagged with the suffix "Rondaxe," the name of a lake just to the north of the mountain, and is sometimes called "Rondaxe Mountain." However, the lakes on the south side of it are the main draw on this short hike. Bald Mountain forms an imposing ridge along the northwestern side of the Fulton Chain of Lakes, which begins at Old Forge with First Lake and flows through eight lakes en route to Raquette Lake. The Fulton Chain is a popular canoe route. From Bald Mountain you can see most of the Fulton

Chain. It is a classic short mileage/big reward hike, perfect for young children. For a modest effort, you get a fun, ledgy climb to an open rock plateau and an extraordinary 360-degree view from the fire tower.

From the trailhead, follow the red NYSDEC markers into a hardwood forest on a broad path dotted with rocks and roots.

At 0.2 miles, the trail turns uphill over a length of slab. Stay to the right up the rock, then to the left near the top of the rock to stay on the official route.

The trail continues upward over more roots and slab. Soon you can see Fourth Lake through the trees. At 0.5 miles, you cross a mudhole and come to a broad patch of bedrock and the first big view of the Fulton Chain. Just past this overlook the trail reenters the woods on more slab, then dips across another potential mudhole.

At 0.6 miles, the trail opens again onto another, bigger bald spot with more of the Fulton Chain below you to the east. The trail ducks back into the trees but parallels the steep mountainside above the lakes. The footing is predominantly slab now and continues along ribs of it that test your balance while affording periodic views.

At 1 mile, you reach the fire tower halfway across the summit plateau. Built in 1917, Rondaxe Tower was one of 120 fire towers atop peaks in New York in the early 20th century. Like other fire towers, the original one was built of wood, then later replaced with the steel structure that stands today. The fire watcher not only looked for forest fires but also recorded all airplanes in the region during World War II. The state retired this tower from active duty in 1990. It reopened in 2005 thanks to efforts by the Friends of Bald Mountain, who maintain it for hikers.

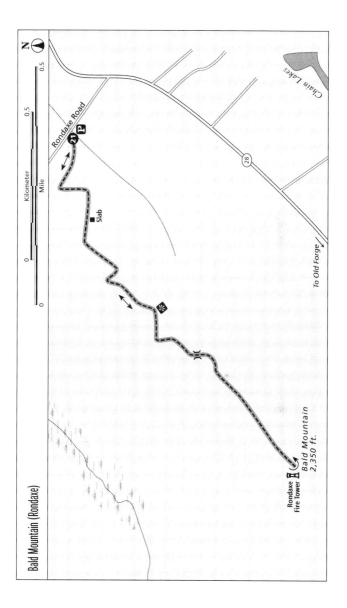

The 360-degree view from the top of the tower is pleasing in all directions, but your eyes will be drawn to the panorama from First to Fourth Lakes below. You can also see the ski trails on McCauley Mountain to the west.

Return by the same route.

Miles and Directions

0.0 Begin at the trailhead, following red NYSDEC markers into a hardwood forest.

0.2 Climb up the right side of a rock chimney, bearing left near the top of the slab to stay on the trail.

0.5 See your first view of the Fulton Chain of Lakes.

0.6 Cross a muddy spot and then come to another (bigger) opening on the ledges.

1.0 Fire tower. Return by the same route.

2.0 Arrive back at the trailhead.

22 Black Bear Mountain

A kid-friendly hike with a fun scramble up a rock chimney and a nice view of Seventh Lake from the summit.

Total distance: 4.2 miles
Type of hike: Out and back
Highest point: 2,454 feet
Vertical gain: 723 feet
Hiking time: About 4 hours

Canine compatibility: Sure-footed hiking dogs only due to the steep rock near the top
Map: USGS Eagle Bay Quad

Finding the trailhead: From the junction of Big Moose Road and NY 28 in Eagle Bay, take NY 28 east 1 mile toward Inlet. The trailhead and parking area are on the left (north) side of the road.

From Arrowhead Park in Inlet, go 0.9 miles west on NY 29. The trailhead and parking area are on the right. **Trailhead GPS:** N43 45.848' / W74 47.632'

The Hike

Located in the Moose River Plains Wild Forest at the northeastern end of Fourth Lake, Black Bear Mountain is named for the bears that are commonly found in the Adirondack Park, though the odds are low of actually seeing one on this hike. Bears tend to avoid humans, especially if you are in a group and talking.

Black Bear Mountain shares its trailhead and parking area with Rocky Mountain, a shorter more popular hike. The less-traveled route up Black Bear Mountain leaves from the far right (east) side of the parking lot, following the yellow NYSDEC markers. The trail is broad, smooth, and easy to follow. It is a ski trail in the winter. It is not open to motor vehicles.

At 0.3 miles, you cross a short footbridge over a seasonal streambed. It's muddy here after a rainstorm.

The trail becomes more cobbled as it climbs parallel to a stream on your left, but it soon departs from the stream, and the grade eases again.

At 0.5 miles, you come to another mudhole with another steep pitch just beyond. The trail has eroded to the point that it feels like you're walking up a streambed. The old logs embedded in the trail help stabilize it.

The path levels and gets smoother again, then at 0.8 miles, you come to a fork. The Northerly Trail departs to the left. Bear right on the Southerly Trail, now following blue NYSDEC discs. There are no names, only arrows, on the trail signs at this junction. In theory, you could make a "lollipop" hike going up one trail and down the other, though finding the Northerly Trail off the summit is not obvious, which is one of the reasons this hike, on the Southerly Trail, is described as an out-and-back route. The other reason is because of what lies ahead.

The ascent up the Southerly Trail turns uphill in earnest, though you get some reprieve at 1 mile, passing through a fern-carpeted clearing. Just beyond the ferns, slab intrudes onto the trail from the right, then you traverse another mudhole, this time aided by a bog bridge and a few strategically placed stepping stones.

At 1.3 miles, another footbridge takes you over a seasonal streamlet before heading up another streambed-like stretch of rough trail. The path dips to cross another seasonal stream, then winds up more washed-out sections. Along the way, you pass several impressive old hemlocks and yellow birch in the forest mix.

At 1.9 miles, the path is blocked by a 40-foot rock chimney, which skilled hikers will have fun climbing. Otherwise,

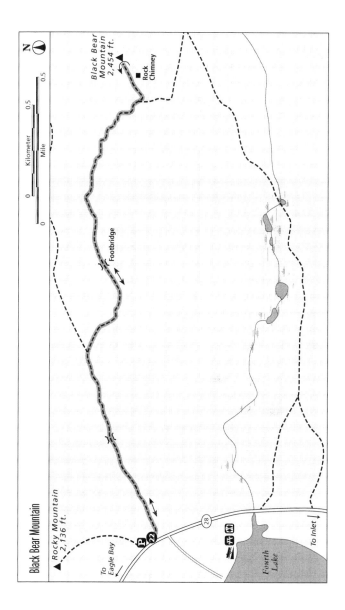

Black Bear Mountain

Black Bear Mountain
2,454 ft.

■ Rock
  Chimney

N

Kilometer
0   0.5

Mile
0   0.5

Footbridge

▲ Rocky Mountain
  2,136 ft.

P
22

To
Eagle Bay

28

To Inlet

Fourth
Lake

turn right to find a rope that helps you up the trickiest part of the rock.

Above the rope, the trail bends to the right, climbing up more rocks, roots, and slab. You pass a rustic railing on your right. The railing makes a 90-degree turn, pointing the way and keeping you on the trail. After scrambling up several more rock chimneys, an arrow points to the right. A few steps later at 2.1 miles, you reach the summit.

The top of Black Bear Mountain is an elongated rock plateau with a nice view to the south of Seventh Lake, with Sixth Lake to the southwest beyond a hump of land. The panorama of the nearby lakes, forests, and mountains pleases the eye from a break in the trees at the eastern end of the rock. In the fall the summit area is ablaze with color, from the maples and from the red berries and colorful leaves of the mountain ash.

Return by the same route.

Miles and Directions

0.0 Follow the path on the east side of the parking lot into the woods.

0.3 Cross a short footbridge then climb a rougher section of trail.

0.5 Cross a mudhole and ascend another eroded section of trail.

0.8 Bear right at the fork, heading uphill on the Southerly Trail (blue markers).

1.0 Pass through a fern-carpeted clearing.

1.3 Cross another footbridge.

1.9 Climb a 40-foot rock chimney.

2.1 Summit. Return by the same route.

4.2 Arrive back at the trailhead and parking area.

The Eastern Adirondacks include much more than the popular Lake George area. They encompass the entire eastern edge of the Adirondack Park, a long narrow swath from Ausable Chasm south along Lake Champlain to Fort Ticonderoga, then along NY 22 south to Whitehall on the Vermont border. From there, it zigzags west below the southern tip of Lake George, then continues back to Ausable Chasm along NY 9. While Lake George is certainly a focal point of the region, due mainly to its concentration of visitors, there are many acres of designated wilderness and wild forest with scenic mountaintops and pristine bodies of water to explore.

Because I-87 runs the length of the region parallel to NY 9, the trailheads in the Eastern Adirondacks are among the most accessible in the park, yet these hikes deserve the same respect as more remote regions. Always wear appropriate clothing and footwear, and bring gear, food, and water for the backcountry. And don't forget rain gear and bug repellent!

23 Buck Mountain

An invigorating hike that rewards you at the top with a terrific view of Lake George and the distant High Peaks.

Total distance: 5.8 miles
Type of hike: Out and back
Highest point: 2,392 feet
Vertical gain: 1,980 feet
Hiking time: About 5 hours

Canine compatibility: Dog-friendly
Map: USGS Shelving Rock Quad (summit), Bolton Landing (trailhead)

Finding the trailhead: Take exit 21 (Lake Luzerne/Prospect Mountain/Hadley/9N) off I-87. At the end of the ramp, turn onto NY 9N north. Go 0.2 miles, then turn left on NY 9N north/9L/9. At the next light, turn right and go 7.3 miles on NY 9L through Cleverdale. Turn left at the sign for Pilot Knob onto Pilot Knob Road, which is also NY 32. The trailhead and parking lot are 3.3 miles ahead on the right.
Trailhead GPS: N43 30.561' / W73 37.818'

The Hike

Buck Mountain sits within the Lake George Wild Forest just below the skinny southern end of Lake Champlain on the shore of Lake George. It's a relatively easy hike despite the nearly 2,000 feet of vertical gain because the climb comes in waves, up short, steep pitches with generous mellow sections in between. It's special for the view of Lake George. There are two approaches to the mountain, one from the east from Shelving Rock Road, and the one described here, from the west near the shore of the lake. This one is more popular because of its pleasing views of the lake along the way.

Following the yellow NYSDEC markers, walk around the gate by the sign-in box, which is meant to keep motorized vehicles off the trail. The hiking route begins as a smooth, wide, flat woods road. After crossing another woods road, the trail comes to a fork at 0.3 miles. The right fork goes to Inman Pond via the Hogtown Trail. Bear left (northeast), continuing toward Buck Mountain.

The old rock-strewn road climbs gradually, following a tributary of Butternut Brook on your left. It bends left (north), crossing the tributary, then winds up through a stand of tall conifers. After a steep section it levels off again. Many large rocks and boulders are scattered in the woods on the hillside to your left.

After a cube-shaped glacial erratic beside the trail, the path passes an old stone wall similar to the mortarless stone piles throughout the woods in nearby New England. These low barriers date back to the 1800s when most of the northeastern lowlands and midlands were farmed or pasture.

The trail soon crosses a stream, then climbs beside it. After a pretty cascade you come over a rise to a junction with another trail to Inman Pond at 1.1 miles. Turn left (northeast), continuing to follow the yellow markers.

At 1.5 miles, the trail comes to a stream. Do not cross here. Head slightly right over a smooth rock outcropping, keeping the stream on your left. The trail bends right, parallel to the stream. At the next level area, cross the stream following a tributary (maybe dry), heading east. Watch for a double marker and the "Trail" sign with an arrow pointing the way. Cross the streamlet, continuing uphill.

The trail soon turns uphill dramatically, climbing up a rocky, washed-out pitch, "the Stairmaster portion of the climb," as one hiker described it.

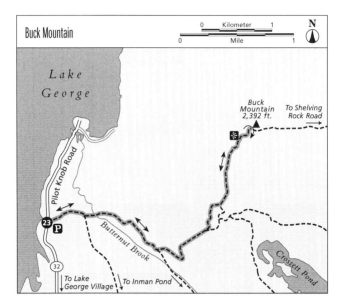

As the pitch mellows, you feel more sun above you and more ledge underfoot. At 2.6 miles, the trail emerges onto open slab with expansive views of the southern end of Lake George. From here, the trail goes in and out of the trees. Follow the cairns and yellow paint to stay on the trail. *Note:* This section of trail is laden with both wild blueberries and a bluish berry on a taller bush. The blueberries are edible, but the other berries are not. If you do not know the difference, don't taste the berry!

Just below the summit, the trail from Shelving Rock Road merges with the trail you are following. Continue straight. The summit lies a few steps ahead, at 2.9 miles. Bear right on the summit slab for an excellent view of the Tongue Mountain Range and the north end of Lake George. From the main summit hump, you look directly across the lake at the Sagamore Hotel, with the High Peaks on the northwestern horizon. The ski trails on Gore Mountain are also visible to the west.

Return to the trailhead by the same route.

Miles and Directions

0.0 Walk around the gate by the sign-in box.

0.3 Bear left at the fork with the Hogtown Trail, continuing toward Buck Mountain.

1.1 Turn left at the second junction with a trail to Inman Pond.

1.5 Head right at a stream, crossing at the arrow.

2.6 Emerge onto open slab and a view of Lake George to the south.

2.85 Continue straight at the junction with the trail from Shelving Rock Road.

2.9 Summit. Return by the same route.

5.8 Arrive back at the trailhead and hiker parking lot.

24 Poke-O-Moonshine Mountain

A woodland hike to a fire tower that passes two pretty beaver ponds then emerges onto a clifftop, with panoramas of the Green Mountains in Vermont and the Adirondack High Peaks.

Total distance: 5.2 miles
Type of hike: Out and back
Highest point: 2,170 feet
Vertical gain: 1,434 feet
Hiking time: About 4.5 hours

Canine compatibility: Dog-friendly. Dogs should be on leash and should not climb the fire tower.
Map: USGS Clintonville Quad

Finding the trailhead: From the north, take I-87 to exit 33, then head south on US 9 for 3.9 miles. The trailhead and large hiker parking lot are on your right (west) side of the road.

From the south, take exit 32 off I-87 in Lewis, then go 8.3 miles north on US 9. **Trailhead GPS:** N44 23.350' / W73 30.447'

The Hike

Poke-O-Moonshine is an anglicized version of two Algonquin words, "pohqui," which means "broken," and "moosie," which means "smooth." It is an apt description of the walls of granite gneiss that rise 1,000 feet from the valley floor. It is a popular spot for rock climbing, though some of the routes may be closed if peregrine falcons are nesting.

There are two hiking routes to the fire tower on the summit and the wonderful 360-degree views. The shorter Ranger Trail departs from a former state campground on US 9. The Ranger Trail climbs a steep, unrelenting 1,200 feet in 1.2 miles. The Observer Trail, described here, is longer, 2.6 miles to the tower but on a more reasonable grade, with the added bonus of passing two pretty beaver ponds along the way. You can make a loop, but to close the gap, you need to walk about a mile on busy US 9.

From the hiker parking lot, follow the blue NYSDEC markers downhill to a footbridge over the north fork of Cold Brook to the sign-in box. Both the stream and the trail curve to the left and are briefly parallel to each other, but they quickly wind apart. The path is wide and easy to follow with good footing as you climb gently through a pretty woodland.

The route flattens on an old woods road as you approach the mountain, but soon tilts upward more noticeably, heading generally to the west. At 0.7 miles, it makes a sharp bend to the right, leaving the woods road, which is blocked by a pile of sticks. After crossing a sturdy footbridge, it meets a woods road again. Turn right on the road, continuing to follow the blue markers.

The trail gains elevation in waves, heading up steep sections, then giving reprieves. At 0.9 miles, while heading up one of these steep spots, you can see a long 20-foot ledge in the forest to your left, the first of many. The ledge soon peters out as the grade mellows for a bit.

At 1.3 miles, you come to a boggy wetland and another footbridge. The bog is just downstream from the first of two beaver ponds. The trail swings around the first pond, then climbs away from it, heading north and climbing steadily, parallel to the stream.

The next steep pitch is more cobbled and wetter in spots, with some slab in the mix, as it heads to the east.

At 1.9 miles, after cresting a hump, the second beaver pond lies on your left. It's a scenic spot, nestled below a dramatic rock face.

Above the second pond, the ascent mellows again, and you begin to see a view through the trees on your right. At

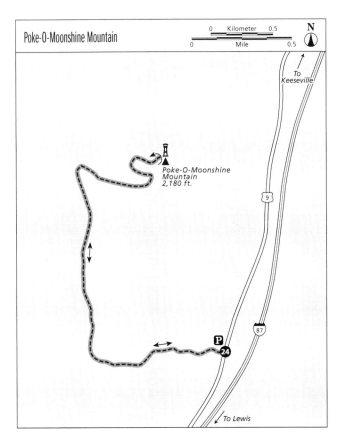

2.2 miles, you come to the junction with the Ranger Trail by a privy and a lean-to. Go straight, walking in front of the lean-to to find the way to the top, following red NYSDEC markers. You'll also pass the remains of the fire watcher's cabin on your right in the woods.

Just above the cabin, you ascend stone steps then wood steps. A short way later, at 2.3 miles, you come to a rock knob and the first jaw-dropper of a view. If you follow the cliff line to your right, it brings you back to the main trail a few steps later, or just retrace back to the trail.

At 2.6 miles, the trail heads up a section of open rock slab through a patch of blueberry bushes. The tower is just ahead.

The original fire tower atop Poke-O-Moonshine was built in 1912 with a wood cabin on top. The metal one that exists today was installed in 1916. It became a National Historic Landmark in 2001. It is not particularly high, and the cabin is usually locked unless a summit steward from the Adirondack Mountain Club or a member of the Friends of Poke-O-Moonshine is present, but the view is terrific nonetheless. Lake Champlain takes up the entire eastern panorama, with Camel's Hump the dominant mountain beyond the lake in the Green Mountains. The Adirondack High Peaks are equally spectacular to the northwest.

Return to the trailhead by the same route.

Miles and Directions

0.0 Begin at the trailhead for the Observer Trail on US 9.

0.7 Turn right off the woods road on a footpath, then turn right when the path meets a woods road again.

0.9 Look for the low ledges in the woods to your left.

1.3 Cross a bog on a footbridge, then pass a beaver pond.

1.9 Pass another beaver pond, this one nestled below a tall cliff.

2.2 Go straight at the junction with the Ranger Trail, in front of the lean-to. Look for the remains of the fire watcher's cabin on your right.

2.3 Bear left, off the main trail, to the top of a rock knob and an impressive clifftop view.

2.6 Fire tower. Return by the same route.

5.2 Arrive back at the trailhead on the edge of the former campground.

25 **Shelving Rock Falls and Lake George**

A unique hike that goes to an impressive multi-tiered waterfall and then along the shore of Lake George with many lake views and spots to swim.

Total distance: 4.2 miles
Type of hike: Loop
Highest point: 590 feet
Vertical gain: 295 feet

Hiking time: About 2.5 hours
Canine compatibility: Dog-friendly. Dogs must be on leash.
Map: USGS Shelving Rock Quad

Finding the trailhead: From exit 20 off I-87, go left (east) off the ramp onto NY 9N/NY 149. Go 0.6 miles past the outlet stores, then turn right on NY 149 east. Go 5.9 miles then turn left onto Buttermilk Falls Road which becomes Sly Pond Road after about 3 miles. Sly Pond Road turns to dirt then becomes Shelving Rock Road at 8.8 miles. The road turns sharp left at the Hogtown trailhead parking lot. Continue another 2.6 miles to the trailhead which is in the middle of the larger Shelving Rock state day-use area, 11 miles from the turn onto Buttermilk Falls Road. Park in Lot #1 on the left just after the bridge over Shelving Rock Brook. The trailhead is a short distance back up Shelving Rock Road on the opposite side of the bridge.
Trailhead GPS: N43 55.192' / W73 59.650'

The Hike

Shelving Rock is a popular day-use area during the summer, so arrive early if you want to park near the trailhead. Parking is only allowed in the designated parking lots, not along Shelving Rock Road, and parking is shared with the trail to Shelving Rock Mountain. Most people go to the falls and turn around, but it's worth continuing to the shore of Lake

George where there are many rocky outcroppings and other perches by the water.

From Parking Lot #1, walk back up Shelving Rock Road then turn right onto the start of the trail, at the far end of the bridge over Shelving Rock Brook. The path is wide and smooth like an old woods road, though it was actually a carriage road built in the late 1800s by George Owen Knapp, the wealthy industrialist who founded Union Carbide. It is part of a network of 30 miles of carriage roads around his former estate.

The route travels under tall hemlocks parallel to the brook. At 0.4 miles, you pass a reedy wetland on your right and begin to hear the rush of water. The top of the falls is just ahead, at an old dam with two large pipes poking out just below the spillover.

Continue down the trail, then turn right following the yellow NYSDEC trail markers to the base of the falls. This is a high-use area with many unofficial trails, so don't worry if you can't figure out the exact way to go. Almost every route downhill takes you to the base of the main 50-foot waterfall.

To continue to the lakeshore, you've got two choices: Climb back to the carriage road or continue along the brook that enters a gorge, which is the route described here. Below the main waterfall, follow the brook to a smaller cascade which spills into a pretty pool. From here, a footpath traverses the wall of the gorge about halfway up it. At 1 mile, it turns uphill but continues to parallel the brook, terracing the steep gorge wall. When in doubt, stay high through this area so that you don't meet an impassable spot. Eventually all of the herd paths converge below a rock outcropping where its "shell" (a big slab) has cracked apart from the main wall of rock. Many interesting trees grow on top of and around the rocks here. Bear left just past the cracked boulder on the higher herd path.

At 1.3 miles, you come to the carriage road again. Turn right on the carriage road, heading downhill. A short way farther, the carriage road comes to the shore of Lake George by the side of Log Bay, then takes a sharp right. A footpath continues to the left. Turn right on the main carriage road, following the red NYSDEC trail markers.

The smooth path is now level through the woods. You sense the lake on your left. At 1.5 miles, the route crosses a substantial bridge over the mouth of Shelving Rock Brook, with a nice view of the lake to your left.

At 1.7 miles, you come to an unmarked junction. Continue along the lakeshore following the red discs. The route soon passes a couple of old privies in the woods and a peninsula on your left. The large island close to the shore is Log Bay Island.

Continuing along the lakeshore, you pass a couple more points of rock jutting into the lake. At 2.3 miles, the point on your left has a particularly nice view down Lake George. From there, the trail turns right, then left away from the lakeshore for a moment. When you are back by the water, the large island to your left is called Hens and Chickens Island.

At 2.7 miles, a rocky point juts into the water from across a short, narrow spit of land. This is your turnaround point. Just beyond, you can see private docks and houses.

To make a loop, at 3.6 miles, turn left at a fork (no sign), heading uphill away from the lake and following blue discs. This trail is more cobbled than the carriage road by the lake, but the ascent is moderate.

At 3.9 miles, the trail ends at the gate by Parking Lot #5 on Shelving Rock Road. Turn right following the road, uphill, to close the loop back at Parking Lot #1 at 4.2 miles.

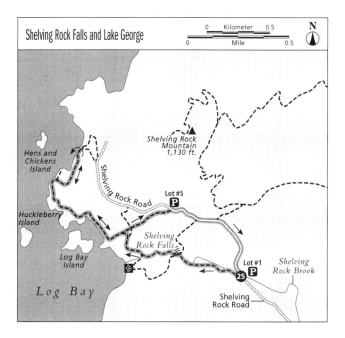

Shelving Rock Falls and Lake George

Hens and Chickens Island

Shelving Rock Mountain 1,130 ft.

Shelving Rock Road

Lot #5 P

Huckleberry Island

Shelving Rock Falls

Log Bay Island

Lot #1 P

Shelving Rock Brook

Log Bay

Shelving Rock Road

Miles and Directions

0.0 Start beside the bridge on Shelving Rock Road where it crosses over Shelving Rock Brook.

0.4 Waterfall. Pass a reedy wetland on your right, then come to the top of the falls at an old dam.

1.0 Follow the brook, terracing the hillside well above it.

1.3 Turn right on the carriage road, heading downhill, then turn sharp right where the carriage road meets the shore of Lake George.

1.5 Cross a substantial bridge over the mouth of Shelving Rock Brook.

1.7 Bear left at an unmarked junction, staying by the lakeshore.

2.3 Enjoy a particularly nice view down Lake George from a rock point.

2.7 Turn around at another waterfront viewpoint and retrace back along the lakeshore.

3.6 Turn left leaving the lakeshore and heading uphill into the forest.

3.9 Go around the gate into Parking Lot #5, then continue uphill on Shelving Rock Road.

4.2 Arrive back at Parking Lot #1, closing the loop.

About the Author

Born in Saranac Lake, New York, **Lisa Ballard** has been hiking, paddling, fishing, and skiing in the Adirondacks for most of her life. She still spends her summers in the Adirondacks, visiting her family, spending time in the backcountry, and enjoying her camp (summer home) on Chateaugay Lake.

A full-time freelance writer and photographer, Ballard's images have appeared in numerous publications including *Backpacker*, *Adirondack Life*, and *Adirondack Explorer*. She has an extensive stock-photo file of the Adirondacks. "If you can see it from a hiking trail, I've probably taken a picture of it," she says.

A past president of the Outdoor Writers Association of America, Lisa complements her visual skills with writing. She has written hundreds of articles for as many magazines and websites, plus a number of books in addition to the first and second editions of this one: *Ski Faster! Guide to Ski Racing and High Performance Skiing, Best Hikes with Dogs: New Hampshire and Vermont, Hiking the Green Mountains, Hiking the White Mountains, Hiking the Adirondacks,* and *Backpacker Magazine's Predicting Weather: Predicting, Forecasting and Planning*.

To see Lisa's award-winning images and to learn more about her work, visit www.LisaBallardOutdoors.com.

American Hiking Society is the only national voice for hikers—dedicated to promoting and protecting America's hiking trails, their surrounding natural areas, and the hiking experience.

At American Hiking Society, we work hard so you can play! We advocate for families who love to hike, and we support communities who are creating new opportunities for your trail family to get outside. Hiking is a great way to bond with your kids, parents, grandparents, neighbors, or even furry friends.

Come with us on the trail and listen to the sweet sound of bird songs and look high into the boughs of old oak trees. We'll help you develop an active lifestyle, learn about the wonders of nature, and become a steward of your favorite trails. So grab your hiking shoes, a well-stocked daypack, partner, kids, friends, parents, and dogs— and get outdoors!